THE CHRYSALIS
AND
THE KINGDOM

Second Edition

THE CHRYSALIS AND THE KINGDOM

Second Edition

Michael Bunch

Library of Congress Control Number:		2006907273
ISBN:	Hardcover	978-1-4257-2939-4
	Softcover	978-1-4257-2938-7

To order additional copies of this book, contact:
Xlibris Corporation
1-888-795-4274
www.Xlibris.com
Orders@Xlibris.com
30262

CONTENTS

CHAPTER FOUR
New Life

FORWARD

We are born into this world unprotected and vulnerable. As we grow we learn much and we are hurt much. We eventually develop defense mechanisms, that are intended to protect us. But not only do they protect us, from time to time they also keep out the loving warmth of the Kingdom. It is my hope that you and the people with whom you share the stories may break out of the chrysalis which imprisons you into the glorious light of the Master's Kingdom. It is my hope that these stories may help you to grow and in a subtle way teach you of the magnificent beauty of God's love. I encourage you to share what you have learned, just as I have and in so doing know the infinite pleasure in giving.

MICHAEL BUNCH
Author
Copyright 1999, 2005 & 2007

CHAPTER ONE

Spring Growth

When winter has passed and there is the coming of the spring we find renewed growth in the brilliant glowing light of each new day. With it will come a rush of New Hope for the coming year. All that is required of us it to bask in the warmth of that day and to drink in the richness which will abundantly flow around us.

THE KINGDOM OF ELAN

It is told in the Great Book of Wisdom by the prophet Melchizedek, many years ago in a kingdom in the far regions of the earth, there lived a mighty King, Leoden the III. He was known throughout the region for his wisdom and his goodness. No one could utter a word against him because he was always kind and just. He was a magnificent man to behold. He was a tall man of 6'-71/2" (which was a remarkable height for the people of the region in that day). He had light brown hair and deep blue eyes that burned with fire whenever he was incited to rage. He carried himself in all things with majestic grace and at all times exemplified what it was to be a good king.

His land was filled with good, upright and just people. They closely followed his leadership, not only in political, but also spiritual matters. Not only was he the political head of state, but he was also the high priest in charge of the great temple of Nema, the capital of the Kingdom of Elan. He took his responsibilities very seriously. All of Elan prospered mightily under his leadership because of the nation's devotion, under his spiritual guidance, to El Shaddi the great God of the heavens and of the earth. In all things the people of the land scrupulously kept his eleven great laws. But most importantly, above all else they never failed to follow his last and most important law.

The ten laws of the great God of the Heavens were written everywhere! They were found inscribed on the walls of all public buildings. They were painted on every doorpost and cut into the cornerstones of all public buildings. They were sewn into banners, written in songs and in every fashion they were steeped deep into the fabric of the society. They were taught in the schools. The elders of the land were constantly expounding on them and extolling the young to live by every one of the precepts, without exception, without reservation. However, the eleventh law was never written down because it was every citizen's responsibility to write it indelibly in their hearts. It was considered of the utmost importance to be kept alive there at all cost. It was far more valuable to the individual than anything that they possessed (even more valuable than their very life). Every man, woman and child struggled daily to bring its words to life in their daily living.

Prosperity was abundant everywhere in the kingdom. The pastures of Elan were filled with fat cattle and the fields of the land always produced tenfold more than any of the neighboring kingdoms. All of the people were well fed and poverty was virtually unknown in the kingdom. Elan was located at the center of the great trading routes of the region. Commerce abounded, because the crossroads of the West and the East met at Nema. There was no need for taxing the people. All of the kings on and near Elan's borders sent great bounty to King Leoden seeking his favor. Such great riches accumulated in the King's treasury that it could not be counted. The King in his wisdom made no formal treaties with any nation. King Leoden wisely avoided them, fearing the entanglements that they would bring and that they might draw his nation into unwanted wars. War could not be tolerated in Elan, since their first law was that no man should kill another. Thus the King skillfully maneuvered around those less wise than he who would secretly set about their profane schemes as they vied for influence in the region. So it was written in the Great Book of Records, which chronicled the deeds of the Kings.

It was also written in the Great Book that on the event of the 25th year of the rule of King Leoden, he issued a proclamation that was to be read in every village of the land. He proclaimed that a great festival was to be held in honor of their God in thanksgiving for the many years of great bounty. Years, which were without wars and without, want. His decree ordered that every citizen of the kingdom observe one full week from sunup to sundown of fasting, to be followed by one week of joyous celebration in thanksgiving to the One Great God of the Heavens for His abundant gifts. Further, he ordered that a mighty 50-cubit obelisk to be raised. On it was to be inscribed the ten great laws of their God and beneath it was to be buried a great treasure (to remain there preserved for posterity).

It is told by the prophet Melchizedek in the Great Book of Records that at the end of the two-week period, on the Sabbath day, as prescribed by the King's proclamation, the unveiling of the obelisk was to take place. It took an incredible toil, all day and all night for two and one half months just to drag the great obelisk to the temple gate from its quarry 350 miles to the south. Its carriage had been built of the finest cedar from the kingdom of Nonabel to the north. The men of the work crews sang as they gladly toiled without rest, dragging their heavily laden sled through the mountains and across the great plane of tears. They stopped only to repair the sled whenever the strain became too great for such a common wood to bare. They labored only with their bodies, pulling the heavy sled, spurning the use of draft animals. They competed with each other for the honor of pulling the sled to the temple Nema. They sang with great joy, rejoicing that their efforts would honor the one Great God of the Universe as they toiled. Soon it was time for the unveiling of the obelisk. The morning had just broken as King Leoden mounted the podium erected in front of the shrouded obelisk. He offered a prayer of thanksgiving to the One Great God of the Heavens saying, "Oh mighty Master of all of the Universe, you have blessed your people much. Though we are a small nation, all of the world comes to our door to bring tribute. You have caused your lands to be bountiful and your people to prosper mightily. It is to You that we give our praise and our thanksgiving. It is to You and only to You that we give all the glory. No other God exists but you, and it is You who is the greatness of this land." Then with a grand gesture of the royal scepter, he motioned to the priest behind him to light the sacrificial fires.

One hundred priests bearing a torch in each hand rushed forward to 400 altars and sent a flurry of sweet smelling incense rushing into the air. The King then handed his scepter to Shalimar, his first-born son, withdrew his golden sword (the kingdom's symbol of justice) from his belt and raised it high into the air. The crowd of many thousands roared their approval as it exploded in a brilliant array of golden light upon catching the warm rays of the morning sun like a glistening multifaceted shard. With one mighty stroke, he cut the ironwood block in half that was holding the curtain in place. As it fell, the priest released 10,000 white doves, that passed over the crowd like a rushing of a mighty wind.

A thundering silence gripped the assembly as the curtain fell to the ground. They were struck with awe. Before them stood an obelisk of such beauty, of which had never been seen on the face of the earth before. It stood 50 cubits tall and was set upon a 15 cubit square pedestal of red granite. It was covered with the finest of white alabaster. It gleamed and shimmered in the morning sun like a magnificent jewel as the clouds danced around its summit. On all four sides were written the ten great laws of the land. Each one was cut deep into the stone, filled with blood red paint and outlined in pure gold. On the plinth at the base was inscribed the letters larger than a man, "BEHOLD OUR TREASURE."

The mighty obelisk soon became a constant reminder of the responsibilities of the citizenry and the people were grateful to their King for having built it for them. For many years thereafter, they told of the greatness of that day and of the great treasure which was buried beneath that stone. With the passing of the years, King Leoden became wiser in his age. His many years of rule were mightily blessed with even greater abundance, replete justice, and completed with abundant peace. Eventually he passed from this world into the next and his son Shalimar became King. Shalimar was also a just king. He worked feverishly to eradicate injustice and to destroy any images of false gods that he found in his land. In doing this he also greatly honored the One Great God of the Heavens. His ten great rules were supreme in the land and the people of Elan prospered.

On the event of the 27th year of Shalimar's reign, a great famine spread throughout the world. But, because Elan was a just land and the Great God to the Heavens loved its people deeply, he had sent a messenger to them to warn them of his impending judgment against the infidelity of their neighbors. It was I, Melchizedek, who thundered the words of the Great God of the Heaven's warning to the people.

Shalimar made great haste as he put away large stores of grain, dry meat and fruits to protect his people from the ravages of the seven-year hunger they knew was to come.

In the first year of the famine, few nations became concerned since the spring rains had been slow to come before. They all knew that the rains would become more plentiful next year. Besides they were confident that their current stocks of grain would hold off the hunger until the rain came once again. When the rains failed to come the second year, the surrounding kingdoms began to rattle their sabers to cover the growling in their people's empty stomachs. Soon they marshaled their wealth and went to Shalimar for help.

The King of Ragida came in person to beg for his people's needs. He cried out earnestly for help, since no other kingdom would sell him grain because he had abused his neighbors too many times before. Shalimar scolded him harshly for his foolishness at not listening to his warnings to change his evil ways. Then Shalimar scolded him for not listening to his warnings of the impending disaster. He was told to return the following day. After consultation with the council of twelve, his advisors, Shalimar then agreed to sell them all the grain that they would require, at half the prevailing world price. During the third and fourth years the Leoden did the same thing. He shared freely with all of his neighbors.

By the end of the fifth year the greatest famine in recorded history had gripped all the nations of the region (except Elan). It had reduced their populations mightily. When the skies refused to give up its bounty again on the sixth and seventh years a spreading panic gripped the surrounding kingdoms. Great dust storms destroyed the once rich farmland and filled the noontime sun with blackness. The rivers of the region dried up and refused to give up any fish. By the second month of the seventh year over half a dozen kingdoms had fallen to bankruptcy or to rebellion spawned of the hapless hunger of their people. The kingdom of Marduk to the north marshaled a mighty army and destroyed Nonabel, burning her capital and killing the entire royal family in one night. Marduk was an evil kingdom ruled by Tiamat who was reputed to be more a bandit than king. He was known for his cruelty and his great treachery. He enjoyed killing and lusted constantly for the taste of battle. His greatest pleasure was in the glory of the carnage of war. He lusted for it more than any other thing in the world.

When Tiamat heard of the stories of the richness of Elan and of the great treasure buried beneath the mighty obelisk at Nema, his heart burned with uncontrollable lust to have it. As Tiamat surveyed his nation around him he saw that his people were also on the verge of starvation (having squandered the spoils of war). His heart hungered for more war and the glory it would bring to him as a mighty conqueror. He also knew that Elan was weak, in fact it had fewer than 300 palace guards to defend all of its 1,850 square miles of territory. Additionally he understood well that the meager spoils of Nonabel's conquest would soon be consumed and that much more would be required to sustain his control over the army. Elan lay ahead of him fat in its richness and virtually undefended. He decided to have it.

The following week Tiamat sent an emissary to the court of King Shalimar demanding food and tribute. Shalimar was greatly affronted by such a rude gesture, yet the kindness of his heart was far greater than the deepness of the insult. He ordered the royal granary opened that a hundred wagons of dry meats and grains to be sent to Tiamat. With it he sent this message: "With our brothers in need we will share all that the Great God of the Heavens has given to us."

When the food arrived, Tiamat reeled with raucous laughter, saying what a fool Shalimar must be and what riches he must have to be able to send to us such tribute. There must be countless wagons of grain in the land; they must have many hundreds of warehouses filled with great riches. When I have it I will possess the power to rule over the entire world. Every kingdom will have to bow to me or starve. All kings must supplicate before me and pay homage to our great gods, the chief among them Mestema.

Tiamat and his people worshipped many gods. But the greatest among them were their gods of war: Sabott, Loggreha, Tardus, and Shairron. It was to them that they cried out with sacrifices of children's lives and slaves' hearts for a good fortune. But to Mestema, their chief god of destruction, they sacrificed twice as much blood to insure swift victories. It was he who would clear the path before them and he who would cloud the minds of the leaders of their opponents (or so they believed) having seen it happen countless times before with many lesser nations.

As the mighty King Tiamat massed his troops on the border of Elan. He counted his host, boasting aloud of his power: "10,000 chariots, 50,000 foot soldiers, 28,000 lancers and 30,500 archers awaited his command. Tiamat rose to the front in his gilt chariot to address his army. "Brethren, we have come forth out of the gates of Shembella a mighty hoard. Out of the gates of our great capitol city Findhorn did we come and we are a mighty army about to set out upon a holy cause. We are the greatest army that the world has ever seen. There is no greater assemblage of power in all the world. Our power is felt from Tyrea in the north, to Pytheria in the south. Our battle flag of victory has flown over Hittites, Seathians, and Cyprians alike. We have conquered all that would not bend to our will. We have crushed Nonabel like the insignificant insect that it was and now we shall reduce all of Elan to ashes in three days. The rich plum of Nema is ours for the plucking. All we must do is march southward and take it. No power on earth can prevail against us; our gods are all powerful. Mestima will lead them before us against our enemies. We are honor bound to crush this insignificant kingdom, to eradicate its heresy against our gods. We must destroy these blind stiff-necked men of Elan lest their beliefs spread like a disease among our lands. Onward," he shouted, "to honor, to victory, and to glory. All honor and glory to Mestema." With that a mighty roar arose from the assembled hoard that shook the very earth. Tiamat raised his banner high into the air and thrust it forward like a javelin hurling it across the border of Elan as a signal to begin the invasion. A loud blast of trumpets erupted, tearing the silence of the cool spring day, as all of Tiamat's army thundered forward in one great rush.

By week's end, Tiamat's troops had spread destruction across the land, of Elan leaving little more than smoldering ruins in their path. They spread across the richness of the land like a hoard of locust, devouring everything in their path. They burned villages, defiled the women, and sowed salt into the fields as they went. On the morning of the Sabbath Day, Tiamat found himself at the gates of Nema.

Much to his great surprise, the gates were open wide and unguarded. Sensing a trap he decided to send a lieutenant and a small body of men into the city to test its defenses. After 2-1/2 hours his lieutenant returned bearing plundered gold in his hands and to report that the city was empty, except for the palace guard and King Shalimar, who held positions at the eastern temple gate near the center of the city.

Excited by the prospect of having the great treasure so easily, Tiamat boasted loudly, "Mestema has honored us, just as I drank the blood of the first dead of Elan from his crushed skull, so too will I drink the blood of Shalimar from his helmet." Tiamat rushed into the city accompanied only by 200 of his personal bodyguards, leaving the great body of his army in the valley outside the city gates. When Tiamat reached the eastern gate of the temple he found much to his surprise, that it too was open and that the mighty obelisk had been toppled. He thought to himself, perhaps a palace coup had occurred. They will soon greet me with the crown and with tribute, he thought.

After a time, as he stood motionless on his horse gazing down at the several large pieces of the shattered obelisk glimmering on the ground before him, King Shalimar addressed him from the parapet of the temple: "Enter the crypt, Tiamat," Shalimar ordered in a loud voice which could be heard echoing mockingly through the empty streets of the city. Looking cautiously around himself, Tiamat dismounted, and entered the open crypt at the base of the obelisk. A few moments later he returned carrying a sealed small plain earthen jar without any marks on it.

King Shalimar glared with fire raging in his eyes at Tiamat as he returned from the crypt. "Tiamat, you would murder the entire world to have our treasure. You have destroyed your neighbors, and defiled our land to have it. And now you would kill me, destroy my people, and lay waste to my kingdom to have this treasure. You would kill so many, to steal it, so I give it to you . . . I go ahead . . . break open the jar." Tiamat stood for a moment in wonderment, examining the plainness of the jar, thinking to himself what if anything of value could come from it. "Break open the jar, Tiamat," Shalimar commanded again in a loud voice, which could be heard outside the city walls by the waiting hoard. With that, Tiamat raised the jar high above his head and hurled it with all his might down upon the pavement at his feet. As it hit the stone it sang out in a high pitched ring as it ricocheted back up striking Tiamat's horse in the temple and killing it instantly. As the dust settled, Tiamat wondered in great amazement how such a frail, earthen jar could do such a thing. Then without thinking his anger rushed out of him bringing with it a profusion of profanity which he showered on Shalimar like a barrage of burning arrows. "Shalimar, I will drink your blood for this insult," he screamed in his blind fury. Drawing his sword he raised it high into the air and crushed the jar with one mighty blow. Upon breaking it open, he found only a small scroll bound by ten golden ribbons. On each ribbon was written one of the ten great rules of the Great God of the Heavens.

After he had removed the ribbons, he unrolled the scroll and read aloud, "Behold our treasure far greater than gold: Koinonia." Tiamat stood motionless for a moment stunned, before this rage gripped him once again as he angrily threw the scroll to the ground cursing. "Shalimar, you have tricked me. Where is the gold? What have you done with the jewels, where is the great treasure, what have you done with them?" His tirade continued for a few moments, then he turned, pulled the captain of the palace guard from his horse and mounted it.

As he did Shalimar called out his name from the parapet. Tiamat turned to catch an expected insult. But instead Shalimar drew his golden sword and threw it swiftly like a spear at Tiamat with a great arcing motion of his right hand, saying with great indignation, "You son of evil, receive your reward, take with you this treasure to your grave." The sword pierced Tiamat's armor just below his right arm cutting into him like a magical shard, piercing his heart. With a shocked gasp, Tiamat fell instantly dead at the foot of his horse.

Great fear struck Tiamat's palace guard as Shalimar walked slowly down the steps of the temple. They froze momentarily in unbelieving horror as Shalimar stooped over the lifeless body of their king, withdrew the sword from his side and cut off his head. As Shalimar raised his bloody prize high into the air, Tiamat's bodyguards panicked. They stampeded in complete disarray from the temple courtyard, down the narrow streets of the city and out the opened gate, which closed mysteriously behind them. They rushed forward in a furry of dust to the tent of Mandragonia, the general of the army. Abyssinia, the captain of the guard, dismounted quickly and rushed toward the entrance of the tent in order to address the general.

But the great clamor had already aroused him from his afternoon slumber and he met Abyssinia at the entry. Before he could ask what had happened, Shalimar appeared at the battlements of the main gate and addressed the great assembly in a loud voice. "You sons of darkness, you daughters of evil, you have come into my kingdom with your King to do evil to my people and to destroy my land. It will not be done." Raising high his right hand, revealing the head of King Tiamat, Shalimar screamed as furry blazed from his eyes, "The great Master of the Heavens will not allow this to be, . . . here . . . take back your accursed King." Then with a swift motion he hurled King Tiamat's head from the wall, which crashed like a ripe pomegranate at the base of the wall. Almost immediately, a great blast of trumpets erupted from the temple. The 350 temple priests blew a mighty chorus of praise to their God, as the head of Tiamat burst on the stones below King Shalimar.

This was the signal the people of Elan had been waiting for. With the trumpets arose a great clamor from the hills surrounding the plain in front of the city. From all directions a great noise surrounded the army of Marduk waiting in the valley. The noise drowned out their screams of fear, which erupted from the army as it began to panic. The wives of Elan clanged on pots and pans as they sang the salvation song. The men of Elan drove a herd of 15,000 oxen, 9,000 camels, 22,000 sheep and 18,500 cattle into the camp from three sides at a stampede. As the animals rushed forward, the troops of Marduk retreated in confusion toward the Plain of Jars. Simultaneously, Shalimar's palace guard sent a rain of fiery arrows into the army of Marduk from their hiding places in the secret chambers within the city walls.

Shalimar and his palace guard chased the retreating rabble first to the Plain of Tears to the North where it was met by a wall of flames as the children of Elan set fire to a line of brush soaked in olive oil. As the leading ranks of the army turned to the west in order to avoid the flames, they fell upon the spears of those following close behind them. In their panic they left 50,000 dead on the plain. When they arrived at the river Reannan, they found the bridges had been burned and were forced to ford the river unprotected. As they entered the water, casting off their heavy armor for fear of drowning, the old men of Elan broke the dams causing the river to rise swiftly sweeping them to their deaths in the Rebus Sea. Not one man nor one beast of the army of Marduk was saved that day.

That evening the citizens of Elan returned to their city from the hills to which they fled, to lay their trap for prayers of thanksgiving. They then spent the next 12 days gathering up the cast off weapons, burning the bodies, and piling high the booty in the temple treasury. I, Melchizedek, testify that these things are true and I have written of these matters in the Great Book of the Kings. It was I who stood at the right hand of first Leoden and then later that of his son Shalimar and witnessed these mighty deeds.

To this day it is told of how miraculously the Great God of the Heavens saved the defenseless kingdom of Elan. Often it is spoken of the courage of Shalimar and the bravery of the unarmed people of Nema. To this day this story is told by young and old alike. They speak with great reverence of the great victory over Tiamat and Marduk and of the great treasure buried beneath the obelisk. They speak of the great wisdom and mercy of the Great God of the Universe. So it is written in the Book of the Kings.

WAR CLOUDS

Jim Stroble was a mediocre student, as was I, when he and I
went to high school together. He never really excelled at any
sport, although he tried. He enjoyed bodybuilding and could almost
always be found in the weight room after classes working out. He
wasn't a particularly large boy nor was he abnormally aggressive, but
over time he managed to develop a respectable physique. His soft
sandy-brown hair and light blue eyes seemed to invite friendliness. He
came from a middle-class farm family in upstate Atwater, California.
His mother and father were good hard-working people who believed
in the traditional American values. They raised all three of their
children, Jim, Audrey, and Anna with a strong belief in God and a
firm understanding of the principles which made America great.

Jim wasn't the most popular guy in the world, but almost everyone
at Atwater High School liked him. He had a particularly gentle spirit,
and despite his powerful build, he would avoid a fight rather than
scrap. On several occasions he was known to step into a fight and
persuade the bully to quickly end the confrontation. This rarely set
well with the "in" crowd, but needless to say, the vast majority of the
students looked on it with great approval, particularly me, who would
have been pounded on several occasions, except that he intervened.

When graduation day came in August of 1968, Jim walked across
the platform in the medium blue gown and cap along with his other
classmates. He obtained a C status and there were no long accolades
for him nor did anyone offer him an expensive scholarship to an Ivy
League school. Nevertheless, his mom and dad were very proud of

him. He was warmly received the next day when he announced that he had joined the marines. Graduation day had come in the midst of the Viet Nam War and the war clouds were gathering in the west for another monsoon offensive. Many young men of that day joined the service to avoid the war, hoping to be assigned to a non-combat position or to Europe. Others dodged the draft, moving north to safer pastures. Still others went to college solely for the 2-F deferment.

Jim chose to join the service in order to fight for something that he believed in. Moreover, he requested assignment to the Amer-Cal Division, who were constantly in the forefront of the battle. It wasn't that he wanted to kill anyone. It's just that he figured he should be among the best and to him that was the Amer-Cal. The big red ONE!

I remember when Jim came home on furlough from basic at Quantico. I had to really bite my tongue when I saw his skinned head. Other than that, it didn't seem that the training had changed him much. He still had that indomitable smile and the unforgettable warmth in his eyes. His stay was short, then it was off to medic training. When he finished training, he was immediately assigned to the 23rd Division at Da-nang. This he regarded as a prime assignment, because it gave him a great opportunity to practice his new craft.

He came home on a short furlough, after medic training school, but I missed him, especially since he was spending a lot of time with Cathy Blasingame, his high school sweetheart. I can't say that I blame him much. After all, she sure was a lot better looking than I am. She was quite pretty, as she had been one of our high school cheerleader. I was delighted to hear that they were married some two years later and now have three wonderful children.

When Jim arrived in Viet Nam, the Tet offensive had just begun. The North Vietnamese had been pouring troops and supplies over the DMZ and down the Ho Chi Minh Trail for months and now the attack was under way. The battle quickly focused on Kashn, an ignominious hill at a key crossroads out in the middle of nowhere in the jungle. The Viet Cong were well organized and they exploded (all at once on every base camp) across the country. There was simultaneous carnage and fury everywhere. Jim is no real hero, but during the next seven days of battle he was credited with saving the lives of 14 men. On six different occasions, he ran directly into the field of fire to drag a fallen comrade to safety. He continued to do this until a mortar round hit near by him, sending him reeling head over heels into a nearby ditch unconscious and bleeding from his ears. When he woke up in Da-nang regional military hospital, the nurse's aide told him that he had a slight concussion but would be all right. She then showed him his helmet with the top half of it blown off and remarked, "You are one hell'uva lucky man!"

Three weeks later Jim was back on the line again. Again without regard to his own safety, he placed himself in jeopardy to reach fallen soldiers and administer first aid. When he was wounded the second time, he was sent to Travis AFB Air Force Hospital to get some rest and relaxation. It was only a slight wound through the thigh but it was enough to get him transferred back stateside. Of course Cathy was immensely concerned and all the doctors agreed that it was her constant visits that speeded his recovery. When he was given furlough a month later, they were married. Having been wounded twice, Jim was given the option to remain stateside for the remainder of his tour, but he Chose to "finish what he started" as he used to say. After a hurried honeymoon and a quickly set up household, Cathy and Jim parted the following December. She as you might expect, was filled with apprehension. She prayed nightly for him and hoped many times beyond reason that he would return to her safely.

When Jim arrived in Cam-Ron Bay, he felt the same apprehension that all men feel when they step into danger, but that quickly passed as he lost himself in the heat of battle. Again and again he risked his life to save those who were injured. When it came time for his tour of duty to end, his valiant record had come to the attention of his field commander, Brigadier General Adams. When Jim was summoned before the general, expectantly nervous, he could think of nothing that a sergeant could offer a general, so it couldn't be he was calling for advice, and he hadn't broken any regulations. He thought, good grief what have I done, am I in trouble . . . . ?

After the general returned his smart salute and went over his records, Jim relaxed a bit. General Adams informed him that Col.

Johnson, the battalion commander, had recommended him for a Silver Star. Jim was speechless. He did not feel that he deserved it for just doing his job. "Sgt. Stroble," the general said, "according to your records, you are credited with saving the lives of 27 men since you have been here and nearly half of them have been while under direct enemy fire. Is that correct?" "Yes, sir," came his short reply, "I guess so; I kind a lost count." "Sergeant," the general said, "I'm going to approve this recommendation." "Yes, sir," Jim said, "but I'm no hero; I was just doing my job." Before Jim left Viet Nam five months later, he was promoted and I've heard that he was awarded an oak leaf cluster to his Silver Star, but he would never tell anyone about it. He just never really considered himself a hero.

Over the next few years Jim and I lost touch with each other. I moved to Texas to go to college and Jim and Cathy moved to Marysville, California, where they had bought an almond farm. It was exactly what he had always wanted. Jim loved the land and wanted to be a farmer. Nut farming was not as intense as other types of farming. But Jim loved what he did and he loved the land. Under his hardworking hands, the farm, which he named "Hill 9 Ranch" prospered. No one was sure why he chose that name. I suspected it had to do with something he did or heard in Nam.

When I got a surprise phone call from him in September of 1979, I was delighted to no end. He was coming to Houston for a convention and wanted to come by for a visit. I picked him up at the Intercontinental Airport three days later. It was wonderful catching up on old times and, I must admit, it felt good to experience his gentleness again. While he was here, he wanted to see the Goodyear blimp (having never seen a blimp before). So we made plans to catch the next launching that Friday evening at 5 p.m.

When we got there, Jim was as wide-eyed as a 12-year-old boy, despite his 30 plus years. It pleased me very much to watch him enjoy the spectacle and I was disappointed for him that I was unable to arrange a ride for him. The tickets had been sold out months before. As we drove back to my home off Interstate 45, we were forced to detour around downtown Houston because of construction on the off ramp I normally used. That meant that we would have to take I-10 around the north side of the central business area and then turn south on I-59 to pick up I-45 again. As we chitchatted about the blimp and I started my exit from 59 onto 45, a 1953 Chevrolet pick-up came up behind me at what must have been near 75 mph. He rode so close to my rear bumper that I could not see his headlights. He then bumped me from behind. By this time I was on the one lane of the off ramp bridge and there was nowhere to go to get out of his way. I slowed to 40 mph to make the turn. That seemed to infuriate the driver. He was acting like someone who was high on some drug or drunk. As the road widened when the bridge emptied on to the freeway (where it opened up immediately into four lanes), the rusty green pick-up quickly pulled to the right and moved close. He matched my speed and then, hurling profane insults, the mulatto driver reached out his window, slammed the camper mirror against the cab of my truck, breaking it and narrowly missing Jim's arm.

He then attempted to run me into the guardrail, but when I heard the clicking sound of my tires against the pavement markers I swerved to my right, hitting his truck in the right front door panel with my bumper. He then accelerated, veering in front of me. In a series of determined left, right, left lane changes, he forced my truck to a stop in the center of the freeway in the left center lane.

Jumping out of his truck, he ran to my door and pulled me out of my cab, throwing me to the ground in a fit of profanity and fury. Jim got out of his side of the truck, jumped over the hood of the other driver's truck and stepped in between us. The mulatto hesitated for a moment as he assessed Jim's big size. Then the assailant threw two swift punches to Jim's face and body. Without flinching, Jim said, "What was that supposed to prove?" The assailant was shocked that apparently that his punches had no effect said, "Man, like that I'm better than you." "Oh, yeah," Jim said, "Okay, now you've proved it, go on about your business." Jim stooped over to pick me up as the other driver stood there stupefied in silence.

Jim could have easily dodged his punches and might have very well have beaten the assailant within an inch of his life. He just brushed my clothes off as the other driver ran to his truck. The wacko driver put it into gear, advanced 50 feet, stopped, then popped his clutch and ramming the front of my truck as it sat dead in the middle of the freeway, in a final gesture of superiority. Then he sped away.

When we got home, I called the police to report the incident. After I was finished Jim and I sat down to dinner. I was amazed at his calmness and his willingness to take the punches without responding. While I was driving home back from the airport the following day, after taking him to catch his flight home, I had time to reflect on the previous night's activities. I couldn't help but remember all the times that he was always helping the small guy, myself included, when we went to high school. I couldn't help but admire his humility and his genuine understanding of life's wisdom, even when the war clouds gathered over the freeway.

THE TOOTH OF TIME

Roxanne and Franklin grew up together in the small town of Cimeron, New Mexico. There really was not much in the valley that is if you don't count the cows. Cimeron is a wild town of rarely more than 50 people. It is situated at the foothills of the Southern Rocky Mountains in extreme northern New Mexico, almost immediately south of the Colorado border. This is especially beautiful country. The gray granite mountains scream up to touch the sky. The tree bare "old Baldy" mountain dominates the sky to the west. Not far from there further west, is one of the finest ski resorts in the area. Angel Fire is renowned for its rugged country and the steepness of the runs. It is clearly not a beginners ski resort, but it was wildly popular with the tourists and it provided a good source of outside income to what would normally be a very depressed community.

The Tooth of Time out cropping dominates the town. It was named that because it looked like an enormous saber tooth incisor sticking out of the ground. Some of the less sensitive young bucks of the town contested this interpretation and insisted that the smaller protrusion at the tip of the tooth looked like a nipple. You can imagine what they called it. It rose some 150 feet vertically above the mountain setting at a precarious angle to the rest of the mountain as if it had slumped and slid backwards a bit. The old timers often predicted that the tooth would one day come loose and come down on the town late one night and crush it into oblivion. Not a whole lot of the towns people gave that much credence, as it had been up there for thousands of years and would be there for thousands more, or so they said.

Almost everyone in the town is associated with the cattle industry. Cattle are king in the foothills and across the prairie near Cimeron. The weather is incredibly sporadic and not conducive to growing crops, other than the most hardy varieties of clover or hay made possible only in the protected valleys of the mountains. Much of the year the prairie is a hard place. It is very very cold in the winter and very dry in the summer. In fact the prairie turns to lava fields not more than 50 miles east and south of Cimeron. The only things that can grow in those fields are grouse and a few scrawny antelope.

The town of Cimeron is nestled against the mountains in the Cimeron Valley, at a spot where the prairie intrudes into the foothills just under the Tooth of Time. The entire town is dominated by the enormous gray granite outcropping. Many a drunk cowboy has on more than one occasion jokingly changed the name to the tit of time while in a drunken stupor. There was regularly a discussion in the town as to whether it looked like a tooth or a breast. This, as you might, guess waxed and waned with the volume of whiskey and whether the person was a regular member of the Cimeron Baptist church or not.

Roxanne Jensen was born the third child of four to Andy and Rose Mary Jensen, on the Lazy "J" ranch about 25 miles as the crow flies west of Cimeron. They, as you might guess, being good people of the earth, were delighted to have this wonderful gift from God come along. These were hardy hard working people, who loved the land and the creatures on it. They did their best to not over graze the land or to disturb the foliage in the valleys. They knew that the edge effect was a vital part of retaining the fruitfulness of the land, as well as keeping the diverse wildlife in balance. They were always careful to protect the land that they loved and all the animals that lived on it. The only two exceptions that Andy made were with rattlesnakes and bears.

Andy would kill a snake if it got too near the house, to protect his children and the chickens, but would rather not mess with them on the open range if possible. Normally he would carefully steer around them if he came upon them on the trail. Now the bears were another matter. They could be very dangerous, especially during the late fall when pickings became slim. There was more than one occasion when he would lose a calf to a hungry bear trying to fatten up for the long winter hibernation. As a matter of course, whenever he saw one he would quickly draw out his thirty OTT six and fire several shots over their head. He always shot close enough to scare them, but never so close as to hurt them, that is unless they were trying to get one of his calves. It all made good sense to Andy. He had to provide for his family and a rogue bear could kill and eat a dozen yearlings in a month. He thought of himself as lucky because he only had to kill two bears over the years.

One was a sickly old black bear that had to be 20 years old or more. It was an ornery old cuss that had outlived, its ability to scrounge for food. It got to killing calves at night as they slept. The a cagey old critter would sneak up on the cows from up wind, so they could not smell him, and pounce before the mother could react. When Andy shot the old black bear, it had killed six calves in a month. This was an intolerable financial loss. That old bear had to go. It was clearly on its last leg and was much too aggressive to safely have around cattle or people. Andy got several of his friends together to lay bear traps. When that did not work, he organized a hunt with several of his neighbors. The dogs found the bear's den after about four hours of tracking. They smoked it out with burning juniper branches and shot it as it charged the dogs gathered at the opening of the den. Afterwards they skinned it and divided the meat. It was pretty rough eating, as that old bear was pretty scrawny and very tough.

The following year there was trouble with Cindy. Cindy was a 2-3 year old bear who raided the garbage dumps behind the rancher's cabins. This is generally not a problem until it got out of hand. Cindy grew quickly and was nearly 450 pounds by the end of the third summer. They called her Cindy because as an immature bear she would not turn black for five years or more and she was a beautiful cinnamon blond color. She sort of looked like a giant yellow teddy bear, but much more dangerous, of course.

No one thought much of Cindy until she started to get too familiar with the ranchers. In August of that year John Wheelwright had his cousin from Denver, Jacob, visiting for the summer, when he had a scary encounter with Cindy. After the entire family had enjoyed a brisket barbecue, Jacob decided that he would stay a bit longer to read a book around the campfire after everyone went to bed. While Jacob was setting near the campfire behind the cabin Cindy, sauntered out of the forest headed for the dump. They suspected that she was attracted by the smell of the barbecue. She walked over to the fire from behind Jacob. She placed her rather sizable head over Jacobs left shoulder and her right paw over his right shoulder, sort of to say, "what you do'n?" Well as you might guess Jacob was somewhat disturbed. He was after all a city slicker. We don't think that Cindy meant to hurt him, he panicked! He jumped up from the log he was setting on and ran screaming back toward the cabin. Cindy was as frightened by the commotion as he was by her. She reared back as he jumped up. In the process she dragged her paw down Jacobs shoulder and back. Her claws ripped his shirt nearly off and left four long red welts down the entire length of his back.

Jacobs's screams woke everyone in the house and nearly the entire valley. He banged so loudly on the door of the cabin that he cracked the jamb. When his brother came to the door he was all a fumble of garbled words, trembling, sweaty and wide-eyed fear. No one really expected that Cindy was anything more than curious at the time. But you could have never convinced Jacob of that. It took nearly six cups of 90-octane campfire coffee to calm him down. He was convinced that Cindy was trying to eat him and there was nothing that would ever convince him otherwise. He had the welts on this back to prove it. More likely the welts on his back resulted from him getting up so fast with a paw on his shoulder. Had Cindy wanted to attack him she could have literally knocked his head off with one swipe of her paw or for that matter bitten him.

It was several months before Cindy returned to the trash burn pit behind the cabin. Apparently she had been as frightened by the whole mess as Jacob had been. Later that year she started to get into more trouble. Late one afternoon, she put the heavy lean on the kitchen door. Now this was no easy matter as it was a one and one half-inch thick solid oak door held fast to the frame by three sturdy six-inch cast iron hinges and a dead bolt. The family had decided to go visit Aunt Millie up the valley for the day. It was a beautiful Sunday and just right for such matters. John had forgotten to take the trash out to the burn pit before they departed and left it under the kitchen table locking the door as he went. Apparently Cindy could not resist the aroma and she made her move just as John returned from the visit. She had crashed through the door and made a beeline for the trash, bypassing four freshly baked blueberry pies on the counter. When John arrived, she was rooting gleefully through the garbage under what remained of the table. Needless to say his wife was not happy with the mess. John went out to the truck and retrieved an ax handle and old hubcap. He rushed up to the long porch at the front of the house at the opposite end to the kitchen door banging on the hubcap. Cindy panicked and charged out the door dragging a garbage bag behind her. John pursued her beating on the hubcap and screaming at the top of his lungs. Cindy had never heard such a strange noise and rushed behind the house with John in fast pursuit. When his wife got up enough courage to see what was happening behind the house, she chuckled as she watched her husband standing at the base of a 65 foot bull pine tree banging on the hubcap and the big bear thirty feet up the tree, peering around the turn, shivering in fear on a bare branch. She mentioned to John that it was a bit odd to see a 165 pound man tree a 450 pound bear and that if the bear decided to come down it would not be much of a fight. John readily agreed and retreated into the house to get his rifle. By the time he returned Cindy had shimmied down the tree and disappeared into the forest. It took John quite a few hours to clean up the mess and after a time the whole incident was forgotten.

A few months later the situation escalated. It was Roxanne's turn to burn the trash pit that evening. She pulled the six over stuffed bags of garbage in a small red Ryder wagon to the dump. The entire assemblage wagon and all was taller than she was. She did not particularly like this chore, and who could blame her. It didn't particularly smell to good, but it had to be done and it was her turn. After several heaves, she managed to pitch the six heavy bags of trash into the pit. She had not noticed that Cindy was already in the pit rooting through the burned out tin cans. She splashed some kerosene on the trash, set a bit of newspaper alight and threw it into the trash. After a moment there was a whoosh and the angry growl of a bear frightened and slightly burned by the flash of the fuel. Roxanne was shocked as the bear charged out of the burning pit and right over her without missing a beat. This was enough for John. That bear had to be destroyed before someone was hurt. By the time he returned the bear had stampeded out of the pit, down the meadow and back into the woods. It was getting late and not wise to track a frightened bear at night so John decided to wait until the morning.

Armando Garza was the second and last son of Alesandro De La Garza who owned a somewhat smaller ranch down the valley from John. Armando also grew up on the land. He too knew the beauty of the mountain valleys and the treacherous Chinook winds which would bring spring to and end and a foot of snow in a single day. He also worked the land with his father, raising cattle in the narrow valleys and steep hill pastures of Cimeron. Alesandro and Armando were also well acquainted with Cindy and her sometimes erratic behavior. On one occasion, Alesandro surprised her rooting through their trash pit. Cindy panicked leaping some 12 feet out of the pit and ran headlong into a fur tree in her attempt to get away. It was somewhat comical at the time. But now that he heard about what she had been up too more recently, he too was very concerned for his family.

Roxanne and Armando grew up together in the mountains of New Mexico. Well as together as together could be when you are separated by a large mountain. They met periodically in grammar school, as there was only one in the vicinity. During Junior High they went to separate schools, because the school district dividing line split Baldy mountain. When high school time came, they were rejoined at Falcon High, because there were not enough students in the school district to fill more than one school, much less sufficient tax base to pay for two. It was in their sophomore year when they began to reawaken the sleeping feelings. Over the next two and one half years it blossomed, much to both their parents' delight, into true love. They had so much in common. They both loved the country, were raised on cattle ranches and wanted to remain in the area after college.

Both of their parents were wise enough to understand that over the years the cattle business had changed significantly. It was more science and less cattle than it had ever been before. So they encouraged their children to go to college. It was not easy, as college has always been expensive. But Roxanne did exceedingly well with her academics. She was offered and accepted a scholarship in animal husbandry at the University of New Mexico in Clovis. Alessandro was also quite intelligent. He too received a partial scholarship to the Colorado School of Mines in Boulder Colorado. Here in lies the immediate problem. Would their love last through the strain of the 350 miles and four years of college separating them? Both sets of parents were skeptical. But Alessandro and Roxanne swore that it would last.

But as you might guess their love knew no bounds. Both of them were highly committed, much to their parent's surprise. Mom's and Dad's everywhere are alike. They think that their children are always much too young for a relationship and more often think it is sexual infatuation more than love. Certainly to some extent they are right. After all, love does have that component (and delightfully so one might say!) Roxanne and Armando were more than the usual teenagers in love (so to speak). Despite their infrequent visits over the years, and the break for junior high school, they had grown up as kindred spirits. They were children of the land and children of the mountains. The very essence of the great beauty of the mountains was in their blood. They loved the land almost as much as they loved each other. It is literally and figuratively a match made it the clouds. Their love survived the many dozens of long late night drives across the prairie and through the mountains on weekends and on school holidays. They were, whenever they would get together inseparable. And ain't it grand (as Armando used to say!)

Neither of them could hardly wait for graduation day. They had both promised their parents, who had sacrificed a great deal for them to have a college education, that neither of them would quit until they had a bachelor degree. This was perhaps the only reason that they did not elope and move into the high country hunting cabin. The temptation was very real; they both loved the outdoors so much. As far as they were concerned these mountains were God's Country.

Time at the university was filled with classes and long hours of study. Both Roxanne and Armando had to work at a second job to keep in food and shelter, the scholarships simply did not cover all the necessities. But neither of them minded working, as they had worked all their lives very hard on the land. Roxanne struggled through the catcalls and pinches at the Lariat Saloon as she worked to complete her forestry degree. Armando worked as a cowhand for an old timer on the outskirts of town and he loved it. He was looking forward to graduating with a bachelor degree in prairie management with a minor in geology. They both worked very hard and were looking forward to graduation with great relish.

As time passed there were subtle differences that developed between Armando and Roxanne. Certainly they were both still very much attuned to the grand beauty of the American wilderness. But over time, Armando became a little radicalized. I guess it had to do as much with the attitude in the department at the college of mines than anything else. Who knows for sure, but Armando became a radical environmentalist. He had developed in some respects into an outright fanatic.

This was the only thing that Roxanne and Armando would fight about. She would always take the middle ground and he the extreme. After a time, Armando began to dress in the radical style. He grew his hair long and a full beard much to his father's disappointment. Although he never went for the hippie beads, his cowboy hat was tattered beyond all cowboy respectability, as were his jeans and faded shirts. It seemed the longer he stayed at the Colorado School of Mines, the more radical he became. His parents were very concerned, and they even thought that he might join PETA (anathema for rancher.) There was even a rumor that he wanted to become a vegetarian. That would have been the last straw with his father a dedicated cattleman. No one was for sure that was the case, and Armando was wise enough to side step the issue when it came up. Roxanne was also concerned, but she could see past the passionate rhetoric and into his heart, where she found the gentile love still alive. That was enough for her.

They graduated at the end of August, to the great delight of both of their parents. Armando's parents were particularly gratified to see their son comb his hair, roll it neatly and stuff it under the graduation mortarboard. He even trimmed his wild beard. There was hope for him yet they said! Roxanne was on cloud nine having graduated the week before, when at the end of the runway he presented her with a wedding ring and a proposed date in mid-September. It was all she had hoped for and more.

They both returned home after the graduation ceremony with reinvigorated excitement for life. Things were going well and beyond everyone's expectation, Armando landed a job with the New Mexico Wildlife Service. It was more than anyone could have asked for. In fact to make it totally unbelievable he was assigned to the Northern NM sector with its headquarters in Roswell, only a hop skip and a jump from home. It was wonderful, it was perfect it, was unbelievable. It was just great!!!!

When the newness of having the children back in the house again wore off, both Roxanne's and Armando's parents started complaining about Cindy. Apparently, she had become more aggressive in her old age. She was even thought to have started killing calves. This is, as you might expect, an unpardonable sin for a rancher, and for good cause. Cindy was taking the food right out of their mouths and the market for beef was slim at best these days. By this time, there was a countywide bounty out on Cindy. She had become a farah and no one seemed to want her around any more.

Armando was not sure that the culprit was Cindy. He used all of his training to find out who or what had been killing the calves. It took him better than a week and a half to put the story together. A great deal of time to unravel the embellishments of the storytellers who tended to exaggerate the story in their excitement. Perhaps some of it could also be due to old eyes and poor glasses. The facts on the ground did not seem to support the conclusion that all the ranchers had reached. The paw prints they found were simply too small for such a mature bear. Armando concluded that it must be a rogue range bear that was moving into Cindy's home range. Fecal samples around Cindy's den at the base of the Tooth of Time Rock, indicated that she was eating berries, garbage and grubs, like good bears should. There was no indication of her eating meat.

When Armando brought this news to the attention of the county sheriff he simply did not believe him. After all, Cindy had been a pain in the neck for years. She had been shot at a dozen times, but managed to make it out of the garbage pits and into the woods unscathed. They all assumed that she was no longer afraid of men and his guns. This made her dangerous. She had to be destroyed. There was no alternative! Nothing that Armando could do would convince them otherwise.

Armando was deeply troubled that a magnificent creature like Cindy was to be killed on such assumptions, especially when he had the proof that another bear was responsible. He thought it was utterly irrational. He talked it over with Roxanne, who was inclined not to agree with him. She still remembered being run over by that stampeding bear, it left a strong mark on her memory and she was still a little afraid of Cindy. But to avoid an argument, she decided to simply smile and nod. This was not a good time to argue over an issue she knew she could have no effect changing Armando's mind. So she did not even try.

The next morning, the county bounty hunter arrived at Armando's father's ranch with his hounds and two dog handlers. Armando was less than pleased. They asked his father for his assistance in finding Cindy's den. Armando's first instinct was to say something very rude and wish them away. But as is the custom in Armando's family, you never argue with the wishes of your father. He had already agreed, without consulting Armando, that he would help locate the offending bear. Armando was both angry and saddened by this turn of events. But he was honor bound by his family name to help.

Roxanne had come along, because the county bounty hunter was her uncle, and well she sort of wanted to be sure that Cindy was, how shall we say it, dispatched! She smiled and made like she wanted to help Armando. Her feeble smile gave her away, and Armando was deeply hurt, but he did not say anything about it. This was neither the time or the place. Perhaps later, he thought to himself.

It was not long before the pack mules were lead from the trailers, loaded with the supplies and the riding animals saddled. The crew of five made their way up the Indian Creek trail, carefully picking their way through the large boulders that were strewn on the floor of the steep valley. Armando hoped to be first to find the offending bear, if by chance. So he led them away from the Tooth of Time trying to buy a little time. The trek was extremely arduous. There are few if any trails, other than deer trails. These mountains are very steep. They wandered for two days looking for bear sign. The county bounty hunter began to get suspicious, when Armando started tracking the trail of a bear that had to be much too small to be Cindy. He had heard the stories and knew that she was a large animal and could not have made these tracks. Armando was sure that he was on the trail of the marauding animal. But when he lost the trail at the tree line on Old Baldy it was time to turn around. Armando was hoping that they would not find any other tracks. But as luck would have it they almost immediately found larger tracks that turned out to belong to Cindy.

The bounty hunter was excited to finally, after all these days, to find his quarry. He took the lead and started tracking Cindy on his own down the mountain and toward the Tooth of Time. Armando knew that there was little that he could do to dissuade the bounty hunter. It looked like Cindy's days were numbered. It took another three days for the bounty hunter to find her den. And it was not easy as they trailed her along the mountain peaks for nearly 25 miles. It was a rugged trek, in fact it is often joked that these mountains are all UP and there is never enough Down for anyone to enjoy the trip.

It was getting colder, as the winter seemed to be coming on a bit faster than usual this year. As they broke out to the tree line they spotted the cave at the base of the Tooth of Time. Since Cindy was down wind of them, she quickly retreated up a dead pine tree (knowing that there surely must be danger) as she had never smelt humans this high up on the mountain. That and the incessant yelping of the dogs panicked her into treeing so close to her cave. Normally she would never do that. Armando tried one last time to reason with the bounty hunter. But no luck, he had his mind made up to kill that bear and that is what he was going to do.

The hunter was delighted to have it so easy. After all they expected to have to smoke her out of the cave. It was very close to hibernation time and that was not going to be an easy endeavor. Cindy was perched on a dead branch about 35 feet above the ground shivering like a wet puppy from fear. She peered around the trunk of the tree not knowing what to do with all the noise that the dogs were making. She was frantic to get away and had no where to run. The hunter took his thirty OTT six out of the saddle scabbard and walked around the tree to get a better shot at her. Armando turned away, with a small tear in his eye. Roxanne held the horses and did not look, although she wanted to.

The hunter and his two assistants had their hands full. The 30 odd dogs were yelping and jumping up at the bottom of the tree. They could barely gather them together so that the hunter could get close enough to make a clean shot. After a few moments they managed to collar all the dogs and pull them back fifteen feet or so. The hunter had what he needed, a clear shot. Just as he took aim, Cindy shimmied around the tree and perched on a lower branch so that the tree trunk was between her and the hunter. The hunter made a few unprintable comments, as he had to adjust his position among the boulders and re-aim his rifle. Cindy just did not seem to want to cooperate. She seemed to sense what the hunter was doing and would move around the tree keeping the trunk between her and the hunter. There just did not seem to be a easy shot. After a few moments of jockeying for position, the hunter began to lose his patience. He cursed at the bear, just as the branch she was perched on let out a large crack. Cindy grabbed the trunk of the tree with he front paws as it sagged. The noise and motion excited the dogs even more. They all seemed to lunge forward at once breaking free of the handlers. The hunter was engulfed in a sea of barking dogs. They jostled against him with such force that he inadvertently let off a round which struck the tree below where Cindy was perched. Cindy flinched and tried to climb higher on the tree. That was all that was needed for the limb to break. She lost her rear footing and hung momentarily scrambling for traction, before she first slid down the tree and tumbled head over heels to the ground, landing in a sea of angry dogs all barking at one time. She quickly regained her footing, took a wild swing at the mass of dogs sending two of them flying uncontrollable into the brush, injured. She had, unfortunately, for the hunter, managed to land squarely on him as well knocking him unconscious.

There was little that could be done, as Cindy was furious at the dogs and was being bitten all over at once. She probably did not even know that she had landed on the hunter at all. When she bolted for

the cave, there lay the hunter out cold with a broken leg, bruised ribs
and a large gash on his forehead from the rock he landed on. The dog
keepers were busy trying to recover their dogs before the bear hurt any
more of them. Armando had closed his eyes and Roxanne had turned
away. Before anyone could get a word out of the stunned hunter, it
was assumed that Cindy had mauled him. Now it was personal.

Julio, the first handler picked up the hunter's rifle and headed up
the mountain toward the den. Armando caught up to him and warned
him that the Tooth of Time was unstable and that perhaps he should
not go to close to the den. Julio was a bit skeptical but Armando
explained that the large tooth shaped 150-foot tall elliptical rock was
all that remained of a volcanic stem. He explained that over the years
it had worn down to that small edifice and that it was underlain with
very soft limestone, which was quite rare in these granite mountains.
Armando was concerned that if they shot into the cave it all might
come crashing down. He convinced Julio to hold up and wait out the
bear. She would get hungry after a while and would come out of the
cave. Then they would have a good shot.

So they gathered the dogs and calmed them down. They retrieved
the two who were injured and bandaged them. The hunter had his leg
splinted and passed out again without saying a word. It was getting
very late in the afternoon; in fact night had nearly fallen in the valleys
so it would be dangerous to try to make the trek of the mountain
until daybreak. It was decided to build camp right there on the spot.
After all there was plenty of firewood under the old tree now. So that
is what they did. The all agreed to take turns guarding the cave to be
sure that Cindy did not come out as a few stones crumbled down the
mountain side from the tired old Tooth. The spring thaw had taken
its toll and perhaps Armando was right. Armando knew that most
likely Cindy would not come out of the cave until morning, so he
volunteered to take the last watch. With that they cooked a warm meal
of mulligan stew made from a ground hog they managed to shoot
earlier and pemmican. Roxanne brewed up some stiff coffee too. They
settled down for the night and waited for the morning.

The first watch was uneventful as Armando expected. The second
was more tense as the second dog handler expected the bear to rush

him from the dark and maul him. But that was more imagination than fact. When Armando arrived to relieve him, he was so startled that he let off a round which ricocheted off the Tooth sending a cascade of stones down upon the camp. This convinced them to move the dogs, horses and mules a quarter of a mile down the mountain to a safer location. This task fell to Roxanne, who gladly agreed to do so, wanting to get away from the trigger-happy guards.

Armando knew that if he was going to save Cindy he had to do something tonight. He decided to go into the cave to prove that she was not dangerous. He bided his time. Along about 3:30 in the morning he crept up to the cave humming Amazing Grace softly to himself. Perhaps he was not as sure about Cindy as he made out to be. But the gentle humming sound also warned Cindy he was coming so that she would not panic again. He walked slowly into the cave until his flashlight found Cindy cowering in the back of the cave, still shivering from fear. He was careful not to shine the light in her eyes and he talked softly to her like you would talk to a small child. Cindy seemed to calm down a bit and after a few moments Armando sat down on a rock outcropping five feet from her. He pulled out his harmonica and began to play Amazing Grace to a confused, but calm Cindy.

The sound of the music coming from the cave got the dog handlers attention. Sound travels quickly in these tight valleys. It bounced from peak to peak and for a time was hard to locate, as the wind tended to change direction from time to time and disorient the listener. By the time the location of the music was found, it was sun up. Much to everyone's surprise, Roxanne concluded it was coming from the cave. Sense a bear could not play harmonica and Armando was missing, they assumed it was him in the cave playing the slow soft music.

After a few moments all three of them made their way to the south side of the cave and were listening intently. What they did not know was, that the hunter had also awaken and was making his way up to the cave broken leg and all. After a few moments the music stopped and Armando came out of the cave with a big smile on his face, having made his point or so he thought. Everyone was stunned to see him and Cindy, following him like a large puppy as he moved out of the shadow of the cave's overhang into the sunlight. The hunter, not quite knowing what was happening, saw the bear close behind Armando assumed the worst.

He took the rifle that he was using for a crutch and drew it to his shoulder. He let off a round, which exploded with violent noise all around everyone. Cindy instinctively ran back into the cave. Armando froze, stunned. The shell hit up and to the left of his right ear and ricocheted into the cave. This was all that the cave's overhang could take. It began to crumble around him. A large piece fell at his feet, causing him to larch backward into the cave as the entire Tooth started to slide down the mountain in a cascade of loose stones. The limestone was crumbling like chalk. All Armando could do was to follow Cindy into the cave and hope that he would be dug out later. Everyone else ran diagonally down the hill in a westerly direction, hoping to get away from the landslide. The cascade of rocks sent the mules and horses scattering to the winds and loose dirt and rocks buried six dogs. The rest of the dogs scattered in a dozen different directions.

When the dust had settled and all heads counted everyone was ok except Armando who was now sealed in the cave. Roxanne panicked knowing that either he was crushed outright or that he would die of starvation before they could dig him out. Digging him out was impossible, or it seemed. The entire tooth and slid 45 feet down the mountain and covered the opening to the cave like a big door. For all they knew it had crushed the cave as well. After several minuets of trying to call through 50 feet of solid granite it was decided to go for help. Roxanne refused to leave, so the hunter decided to stay with her as the dog handlers went for help. Everyone except Roxanne knew that there was no hope for Armando. It was going to take too much time to get help and return. And even if they could bring the equipment to the 11,000-foot elevation, which was impossible due to the lack of roads. And how in Gods name were they going to move the 250-ton rock?

By the time the rescue party arrived two more days had passed and Roxanne understood that no hope remained. If Armando had not been crushed certainly the bear would get him. There was little more that could be done except to carry the injured hunter back to town and weep. Everyone was sure that they had ended the calf killings, and that gave Armando's parents some consolation.

No one had the heart to tell them that they had continued on the other side of the mountain for anther four months until a scraggly old male black bear had been tracked and shot.

Over time the wounds healed and Roxanne remarried. She never forgot how Cindy had been trapped that day and she never forgot how brave Armando had been to go into that cave to save a guiltless bear. He sacrificed his life for what he believed and that was good. Some of the old timers even said that he saved the town that day because the rock fell back against the mountain rather than falling on the town. It is also said that on lonely nights that you can still hear the sad sound of his harmonica.

THE LEGEND OF
WATCHTNA'S SON

For many years the Cree people roamed the Eastern Mountains of North America. They were a proud people well versed in living in harmony with nature. They fished and collected the fruit of the trees. They hunted the deer, wild birds and the great elk. They gathered the acorns and berries, which grew in abundance around them. The Great Spirit was good to them because they were a just and honorable people, who loved peace and avoided war. The bounty of the land provided them with all their needs. And they were immensely wealthy and prosperous as a people.

Some 430 years ago there lived a woman of the Cree tribe. She was the most beautiful of all women who had been called by the name of the Cree. Her hair was rich and full. Its deep brown color flowed over her body as though it were alive. Her skin was unblemished and flush with a rich color born of the sun. Her arms were strong and the wisdom in her heart was deep. She worked hard and loved her people. Her name was Watchtina. Though her lineage was poor, because her clan was weak, many braves sought her for a wife because she was beautiful, strong, could produce many strong children and she could add to the wealth of their clan.

When her time came to take a husband, many followed her seeking to catch her moccasin. They thought to buy her with many gifts to her brother. Yet she spurned their gifts for wealth was not what she desired. At the tribal council her brother threw away her moccasin, as was their custom at a betrothal. The many young bucks around the fire fought feverishly for her. But in the scuffle, the moccasin and that right to claim her as bride slipped from their fighting hands and landed in the flames. This was a very bad omen, which no brave would dare to battle against as it came with the curse of bareness. After some moments one young brave, one not so strong nor so handsome ran from outside the circle and leaped into the flames snatching the moccasin before it was completely consumed. He jumped out of the fire quickly holding the still smoldering moccasin. Much discussion followed in the council, as all knew that it was now his right to claim Watchtina as his bride.

Watchtina looked deeply into his eyes with apprehension. The young brave walked close to her and handed back to her the remains of her smoldering moccasin. A great gasp arose from all those assembled, as this was greatly unexpected. This returned the choice of whom she would marry back to her. Great confusion erupted with murmuring because it had been many years since anyone returned a moccasin to a maiden. Watchtina too was also confused. She looked about herself and then back to Nechitee who stood in front of her covered with soot smelling of fresh smoke. She hesitated briefly then returned the moccasin to him signaling that it was he that she chose for a husband. Again great clamor arose from the tribe not knowing why she would choose such an ugly skinny man. Watchtina ignored the noise and gently brushed the soot from Nechitee's face. He beamed with a great smile. She knew that he would be a good and honorable husband as he had prized her so much as to give her back her moccasin. That night they became husband and wife according to their custom. For many moons the people of the Cree would talk of that day when the most beautiful squaw would chose such a man of small stature from such a weak clan.

Watchtina of the Dove clan and Nechitee of the Deer clan lived the next four years in great happiness. Watchtina would bear him three healthy sons. They all would grow strong and wise in their parent's image. All three would bring their parents honor among the tribe because they knew well the lesson of their parent's love, which their mother had shown. They also learned the shrewdness that their father lived. He was very wise in the ways of the forest and he understood the gifts of the animals who would surrender their lives so that brother Cree might live. He taught them how to make arrows, how to track a fox, and how to catch a big fish with a whittled twig. He showed them how to find water on the prairie by watching the mud finch's fly to and from the water hole as they built their nest. He was a good father and he spent many love filled hours with his sons teaching them the way of the land.

The Cree people prospered mightily but in the fifth year of their marriage the seasons began to turn against the Cree. They had forgotten the Great Spirit in their fatness and no longer spoke to him of their longings. They no longer spoke of the old ways. They stopped telling of the great quest and the stories of glory and richness which was the oral history of the Cree. So in a short time He turned His face away from them. The warring tribes of the North attacked the Cree and carried off their wealth. The next summer was hot and without rain. The greenness of the forest became lifeless brown. The deer no longer roamed its floor and the wild turkey could not be heard singing out their calls. When fall came two months early the men of the tribe knew that the winter would be very long, very hard and very dangerous. They knew that it would demand a great deal of the tribe and that not all would return from the winter into the next spring. This was a time of great sadness in the village.

The elders of the tribe called a Great Council together. It was decided that all of the men of the tribe would go to the North to raid the Pawnee for food so that the tribe might not starve. The women and children were to be sent South to the sanctuary of the soap stone quarry grounds of the sacred pipe stone. A great wailing and weeping could be heard in the camp that night as many braves took a sacred oath not to retreat in battle, guaranteeing them great honor and almost certain death. Among them was Watchtina's husband.

With the coming of the dawn the men and women parted upon their journey to safety and to glory. On the morning of the third day a great wind blew up from the North with it the wind brought the bitter coldness of the winter's first great storm. It came upon the women with such speed and fury that they soon found themselves scattered and lost in a white maze of ice and snow. Watchtina fell behind the main body of the tribe and being heavy with her young children, and soon became lost in the blizzard. The cold grip of winter cursed her every step. The ice was like a thousand knives, each one cutting her skin as they were driven deep into her flesh by the angry wind. The howling wind built great drifts of snow against her path. Each step became more difficult than the one before it. The snow came down so fast as to suffocate her breath. It blinded her eyes so that they could not see. Already weakened by hunger she wept bitterly against the storm as her tears froze against her cheeks. She cried out angrily against the storm because she knew that they would all perish if she did not find shelter.

Late in the evening Watchtina found a large outcropping of rocks where she laid her children down out of the wind. She fashioned a crude shelter out of pine boughs and lined it with moss, branches and leaves. That night they lay there on the snow, cold and hungry longing for the sweetness of summer when the Great Spirit would once again smile upon them. The night was sleepless for her because she knew that she must take hard action to save her children. She was too weak to carry all three of them and they were too young to fight the winter alone. She wept silently to herself asking for guidance from the Great Spirit. With the rising of the sun she shared her last bit of pemmican with her children and gave the last of her milk to her baby. She lined the niche in the snow with her buffalo robe setting her 16-month-old baby on it and placing her 3-year-old son at the opening side to guard him. She then covered them with boughs and heaped snow against the open to keep in them warmth. After cutting a small air hole in the snow she wrapped her 2 year old son in her blanket and tied him to her back. The wind had slowed some by now, and the sky was clearing. As she began her journey she spoke softly to the Great Spirit to protect her and the children who were left behind.

After several miles of struggling against the diminishing wind, the weather broke. The snow was glistening white. It seemed to be a fairy tale powder, which was spread over the land. The lodge pole pine stood stark against the sky as frozen white totems glistening with ice in the sun. Watchtina's breath froze in the coldness of the air. It hung there after each breath, as though suspended by some an evil spirit. As she walked, over each drift and over each stone that cursed her progress she thought of her children whom had been left behind. Each cold breath seared her lungs as she fought to breathe. She fell many times, cutting her hands on the ice and bruising her legs. Yet she knew that the raiding party would surely have returned to the winter camp by now bearing much needed food and horses. With each step she struggled against the coldness. Her hands and feet could no longer feel the pain, made numb by the freezing winter air. Soon she found herself at the wintering camp valley's edge overlooking the quarry on the horizon. Her heart was lifted as she saw the smoke from the tribe's campfires. She wept for joy as she began to run down the hill to the valley below. When she came to the frozen creek she cautiously picked her way across the slippery stones, knowing that a fall into the frigid water meant certain death. But in her excitement, she slipped and fell into the water up to her knees.

Oh how she cried out in pain, knowing that surely her feet would now freeze. As she struggled up the bank, she cried out Netchitee, Netchitee my husband, where are you, please help me. I am cold and I have no strength to go any further. In her heart she feared that he would not be there, having been killed in the raid.

When Netchitee had returned from the raid the day before he was greatly troubled not to find his family. He had already been searching for her near the edge of the village. Then when he heard her call and ran to meet her. As they came together, his heart was filled with joy to see his squaw alive, yet he felt sorrow for her, seeing her wet hands and feet. He picked her up and carried her to his teepee, knowing that he must act quickly before she froze. There he laid her down by the fire to warm her. He placed her nearly frozen hands under his arms to warm them. He gathered his warm arms around her and lulled her to sleep. When she awoke, she ate only a few dried berries and spoke to Netchitee of two missing children. He was filled with great sadness and went to the huts of his clansmen to seek their aid in rescuing his children. He pleaded with all his heart and every bit of his strength for their help. Yet none would go with him. The raiding party had gone badly. Little food was found and the Pawnee had fought very bravely. Many braves were wounded and many others did not return to the huts of their wives. With great sorrow, Netchitee went to the great Chief Ninguskookt and the Council. Ninguskookt was also filled with great sorrow. He had seen his people scattered and dying. He had seen them alone, hungry and wailing the death song. He had watched them freeze and he wept for them unable to help.

Ninguskookt blessed Netchitee and loaned him his only horse with which to find his children. Yet he could give no food for he too had nothing to give. He could not go with him as he was old and had suffered a serious wound to his leg in the battle. Netchitee began immediately to try to find his children. Night quickly overtook him, but he knew that he could not stop he knew that his children could not survive more than a day or two in this great cold. Or perhaps, he feared brother wolf would find them before he could. When he heard the cry of the wolves yelping to each other from one side of the valley to another as his heart sank. He knew that the wolf would be his enemy this night. He also knew from their cry that they were still hunting and not yet feeding. His heart was straightened as he hurried down into the valley and up the mountain. Netchitee gathered pine cones and lashed them to a stick. With his knife he cut a pine tree and rolled the cones in the pitch. With the ember in his fire bundle he lit his torch as he searched for the trail left by Watchtina. He knew that the wolves too could see the torch and he would fall easy prey to them should they catch him in the deep snow. He carefully backtracked following Watchtina's words and her foot prints in the snow. Fortunately the wind had only partially covered them, and although they were hard to see he could still tell by the light impression in the snow that she had passed this way. He looked for the broken branches and the marks on the trees she had left. Between these two trails he would to find his children, of this he was nearly certain.

After a time Netchitee walked beside his horse to save its strength as he searched for each broken twig and every slash mark on the trees. Sadly within the hour, the wind began to howl once again. He fought very hard to find the trail. As the night wore on into morning, he found himself at the large stone outcropping. The wind had piled even more snow deeper around the opening of the stone outcropping. He felt great fear of losing his children and at the same time sheer joy for finding their hiding place. He saw the paw prints of the wolves near by as a cold chill ran up his spine. He dismounted his horse fearing the worst and hopping for a sign of life to come from within the cave . . . .

Netchitee dug furiously through the snow with his bare hands until he found the pine bows. He saw how they still covered the entry to the niche, this was good. He hesitated a moment in fear then threw them off uncovering his children. As he reached down to pick up his eldest son, he cried out in pain at the coldness of his arm. He tenderly lifted his lifeless body to him, weeping in hopeless desperation. His heart sank into sorrow as he cried out again and again in pain and in great sadness, for his son had frozen to death. Just as he began to turn away, he heard the cry of his youngest son. With unbelieving hands, he picked up the younger boy. He wrapped him in his blanket to warm him. He fed him a small handful of crushed pinion nuts for strength and then tied him to saddle of the horse. He then placed the body of his older son on horse behind him. Netchitee wept because he knew that Naucketa his oldest had given his life to protect his youngest. As he neared the camp, he came upon a doe that had frozen in the storm. He tied a thong around her and dragged her into camp calling out to the Chief as he arrived.

Oh, Great Chief, I left with great fear in my heart and I return with both sorrow and joy. Take this meat and feed all my brothers. A great cry went out in the village. The men of every clan came out to claim their portion of the meat. Yet not one asked about Nechitee's children. They were all too occupied with their hunger and fear for their own children. Netchitee entered his tent with great sorrow. Watchtina met him at the door with outstretched hands. She felt the sorrow written in his face, even before they embraced. She took the body of her lifeless child into the tent to prepare for the burial rite. She wailed the death song and tore her clothing as was the custom of the tribe.

Netchitee returned to the horse and bore his youngest son in his arms into the tent and placed him on the floor among the wailing. Watchtina turned at his crying and swooped him up to her bosom, weeping with joy. Watchtina and Netchitee knelt weeping, for they were both happy and sad. They were sad that one son had perished in the storm, yet they were glad that the younger was live. They thanked the Great Spirit that their oldest son would never feel coldness or hunger again. They rejoiced knowing that his life was easy now as he rested in the village of the Great Spirit. They were happy because the younger son was alive, as a gift of the eldist's sacrifice. In the passing of the seasons Watchtina and Nechitee would go to the great hunting ground, to commune with the Great Spirit. But the story of their lives would be told again and again around the campfires of the Cree. For they truly had a great love.

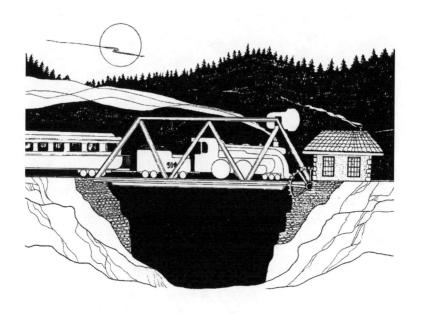

KING'S VALLEY BRIDGE

K ing's Valley is a small town on the upper coast of Washington. It has always been a quiet community of only several hundred people. Not much ever happened of any excitement. Everyone in the town seemed to live a quiet life of leisure and they carried on with their activities almost undisturbed by the passage of time. When the Proctor family moved into King's Valley, no one really noticed them. Jeff, his wife, Elizabeth, and their two-year old son, James, had come there from Seattle some 85 miles to the north. They had had their fill of the big city and were looking for a small town in which to live a quiet life without the pressure of the hurried city.

James was Jeff and Elizabeth's greatest joy and their greatest pride their only child. Both of them had waited late in life to marry and to have children. Now Elizabeth was past childbearing age. So his birth was a welcomed miracle. They loved James very much, perhaps even more than they loved each other. They moved to King's Valley, as much for James, as for themselves. They didn't want their only son growing up in the hard city environment. They had great hopes for him, that one-day he would grow up to do great things.

King's Valley was predominantly a farm community and most of the people who lived in those parts were good hard-working people of the land. They grew some of the best apples in the world, or so they told Jeff. He, for his part, was in agreement, owing to his partiality to fresh fruit. King's Valley owed its only claim to fame to the King's Valley Bridge, which crossed the Tacoma River just east of the town. In the 1840's, the Pacific Western Railway crossed the river there and according to local legend; the last great battle of the Tinglet Indian uprising was fought near the construction site of that bridge. Jeff had been working for the Pacific Western Railway for 17 years. When this opportunity for a transfer came he jumped at it. The operator of the drawbridge at King's Valley had retired and they needed a replacement. Jeff eagerly took the transfer, having already made up his mind to leave the big city. It was just exactly what he wanted. He and his wife looked forward to a little peace and quite in the country. Jeff and Elizabeth bought a cute little cottage with in eyeshot of the bridge and settled down to a quiet life among the magnificent redwood forest. Jeff would take his son with him from time to time as he walked the half-mile to work each morning to relieve Alfred Toller, the night man on the bridge.

Al would normally walk James back to the house where Elizabeth would give him a cup of warm coffee before he drove home to get some sleep. However, this particular morning Elizabeth asked Jeff to keep their son with him that whole day. Elizabeth had some serious cleaning to do in the house and he was constantly getting under foot. Well, since it was Friday and there was no pre-school the next day, Jeff decided to let him stay, even though it was against company policy. James, of course, was delighted to spend a full day frolicking in the snow with his father. Of course, Jeff could not spend all day with his son since he had a good deal of work to do. He knew that a small boy could find plenty to do in the small meadow near the drawbridge, so, when they got there, Jeff went about his work as James ran outside to play.

Along about noontime, the weather began to turn bad. Some fast-moving clouds sped into the King's Valley area and the wind began to blow hard and cold. Jeff put his head out the door and called for James to come inside, just as a call came in from the barge tender U.S.S. Pierce asked for the Rail Bridge to be raised for his passage. The captain reported that he was carrying 151 million gallons of gasoline bound for Seattle. He was in a hurry, being two days behind schedule because of a storm off the coast. Jeff rushed to the microphone and radioed back for additional information. The 12:30 Silver Cloud express from Seattle to San Francisco was due shortly and timing would be critical to avoid an accident. After some chatter, it was decided to proceed, but the captain was instructed to not make more than 8 knots since the river took a sharp turn east near the bridge. Jeff decided it was okay to allow passage of the barge, because the time required to raise and lower the bridge allowed five minutes before the train arrived. Everything would work out fine, he thought.

Jeff looked out his north window and he could see the sun glint of the windows of the train's club cars as it snaked down the mountain switchbacks toward the bridge at a brisk speed. It was still seven miles away. He knew there was plenty of time to raise and lower the bridge for the barge and her cargo. Jeff reached for the control rod and threw it back as the giant gears spun. The bridge began to rise with a groan. It always made a lot of noise, but it worked well, yet Jeff wondered why it was designed so that the operator had to hold the control rod at all times to keep the bridge moving. Maybe it needed repairs, but it was a small nuisance, so he did it. In a few minutes, the bridge was up and the Pierce was proceeding up the river at the prescribed speed.

Then came a garbled message on the pilot's house radio. "May day, May day, May Day . . . This is Captain O'Leary of the U.S.S. Pierce. We have a Class one emergency here. I have a fire in my engine room and have lost power." Jeff could see smoke bellowing out of the port side vents of the Pierce and men running below with fire extinguishers and hoses. Jeff quickly reached over to the microphone and asked about the situation. Captain O'Leary radioed back, "I've lost power . . . will attempt to coast down stream with the current and clear that eastward turn." Jeff could see the tender begin to float slowly back toward the bridge.

He dropped the ship's microphone and grabbed the rail line microphone to relay the warning. By this time, the Silver Cloud was coming down the straightaway at top speed, heading for the bridge. The engineer barked back, "It's too short to stop. I am moving to fast to stop, I'll derail. Get that darn bridge down! I've got 850 passengers on this train." Jeff quickly turned to look at the barge as it floated under the superstructure of the bridge. Just then James came running in the door, holding a half frozen sparrow in his hands and hollering, "Daddy, Daddy, look what I found!" Just as he looked up at his father, he slipped on the wet floor and fell toward the gears of the drawbridge mechanism. The edge of his coat was quickly pulled into the gears. He was held there screaming and crying as he panicked.

Jeff blanched, looked quickly at the train then at the barge tender, and threw the master control handle into the down position. He wanted so much to reach out to his son, but could not because he had to hold on to the master control to keep the bridge moving. As the bridge began to lower, Captain O'Leary barked across the radio, "What are you doing" You're going to crush my funnel." The Pierce just barely drifted past the bridge's superstructure, when it lowered and locked into the down position, crushing James between the gears. Seconds later, the Silver Cloud sped past the control house and over the bridge without incident.

Jeff glanced out the window at the dozens of laughing happy people in the club cars as great tears swelled up in his eyes. When the train had cleared, he sadly went to the gearbox, retrieved his son, wrapped his body in a blanket and walked slowly home. Both Jeff and Elizabeth were destroyed by the tragic accident. Soon there after, they moved away from King's valley. No one is sure where they went, but to this day, the story is still told of what happened that tragic day.

CHAPTER 2

Fatness

After the goodness of spring has been spent we may enjoy the fatness of the summer. It is here that we are then charged with the responsibility to think on what we have learned and to use it to grow in greater depth.

JACOB'S TREE

There once was a large oak tree that grew high in the mountains on the Starns Ranch in Mariposa County, California. It was called Jacob's tree, although no one ever could remember exactly how it got that name. Jacob's tree was unique. It grew where no other tree had grown, in a crevice that was barely large enough for a man's hand. It was different because no other oaks ever grew in that region, at least as far as anyone in those parts knew. Ponderosa pine, Bull nine and Jeffrey pine all grew in abundance. There were multitudes of California spruce and mariposa bushes, but no other oak could be found for hundreds of miles around. It was just too far south and there was not nearly enough water to support a oak. Yet there it stood as it had for almost 2,300 years. How it even got there or even how it survived was beyond anyone's understanding. And perhaps because it seemed out of place and survived in such an alien hot environment, much as Jacob of the old, survived in the desert, is why so long ago it was given its name.

Jacob's tree was tall and broad. Its limbs spread for almost 65 feet in all directions. It leaned at an odd angle to the leeward because the winds were always strong at those high altitudes. It grew, literally, right out of the solid granite. Its roots had cleaved into the stone and shattered it. There it found nourishment in the wind-blown soil, which gathered in the crags. Many of the limbs on the windward side of the tree were gnarled and twisted, and almost half of them had died, being frozen by the yearly winter wind. Over time in order to survive it became necessary for a part of the tree die to insulate the remainder of its trunk from the freezing winds. This allowed the remaining parts to survive the stark winter winds. Jacob's tree's bark was dark gray-brown and scarred in many places. The winds had caused its branches to grow low to the ground. They seemed to creep just a foot or so above the rocks in many places, following the curves in the land. This was truly an ancient remarkable tree.

This particular season a family of doves made their home in Jacob's branches. There was also a squirrel nest in his upper limbs where the squirrel had grown fat on Jacobs acorns. Even a badger managed to claw a small den from the dirt at the base of Jacob's trunk. Together they all lived in harmony, each one depending on the goodness that Jacob gave to them. Every creature of the forest enjoyed the shade Jacob made. His stalwart arms were always a delightful reminder of the Master's presence in the forest. Even the people around those parts grew dependent on Jacob and used him as a reference point.

Jacob's tree could be seen from many many miles around. It stood just below the crest of Proud Horse Mountain. Jacob was much larger than all the trees around him and he stood stark against the shattered gray granite summit of the flat-topped mountain. The top of the tree seemed to touch the very sky. Jacob had a fork in the trunk, which began about halfway down his trunk. Evidently, some hungry deer had nipped the leading bud so many, many years ago, leaving Jacob distinctively marked. Over time the branches filled in the open space, but you could still see the fork at dusk when the last rays of the evening sun silhouetted the tree against the night sky.

When Jacob was young, things were very different. Man was rarely seen in these mountains. The rain came more often then and the sun was not as hot as it is now. But there was always the wind, which was brother, with Jacob and the mountains. For many years they all lived in peace together. But nothing remains unchanged forever. The Pacific Western Lumber Company bought the Starns Ranch when old man Starns passed away; leaving it to his son whom did not love the land and decided to move to the city. Now it was decided that the whole area was to be clear-cut to make way for a new stand of sugar pine for the paper mill. It is difficult to understand why anyone would want to cut such a magnificent tree, much less, plant new sprigs in such a difficult spot. But that is what they decided to do.

Early on the morning of the 25th of June, the peace of the forest was shattered by the sound of heavy equipment and roaring chain saws. Three-and-a-half weeks later the lumberjacks had worked their way to the base of the mountain. The foreman went ahead up the mountain to scout the timber for his report back to headquarters. When he ascended its slopes, marking the trees to be cut and found, Jacob's tree, he was excited by the prospects of so much lumber in one tree so he marked it twice. Besides hard wood always brought top dollar. There had to be at least one-quarter of a million board feet of usable lumber in that tree, he said to himself. Later he gave special instructions to fell it just right, unless it slide down the mountain and be shattered on the rocks. If it did it the wood would fragment and it would become useless.

When the day came to fell Jacob it was a particularly blustery day. The logging crew had worked well into late afternoon before they reached this mighty giant. By this time they were hot and tired so they paused in Jacob's shade to rest for a while. In no time the wind began to pick up as clouds began to gather around the peaks of the adjacent mountains. The foreman could see that a summer lightning storm was gathering. As the thunderhead built up to the east and moved towards them he motioned for everyone to get to work. He cranked up his saw and began to cut the tree before the rain started or the wind picked up too much. In about an hour Jacob's mighty trunk had been ripped open and a large bite was torn from his eastern side at about five feet above the ground. The foreman drove a steel wedge into the cut, intending to lay the tree down neatly in a smooth spot near the crevice where it grew. Just as he struck the final blow with the sledge on the wedge, a rainsquall hit with unexpected intensity. The wind whipped up to 45 knots, turning Jacob so that he twisted northward and fell downhill into the rocks. When he hit, the foreman knew that it was useless to try to recover any lumber. Jacob broke into twelve large pieces, shattering his mighty trunk parallel to the grain in three spots, putting a deep gouge into the main trunk and breaking both of his largest limbs in several places. There he lay, almost as stately as he was before they had cut him down, except now he was dying (after having lived such a long time). When the crew moved on, not much was said. After all, this is what they did for a living.

About a week later, Anthony Harbor, an amateur scientist who lived in the area, heard of what had happened to Jacob's tree. He simply could not let Jacob's tree die without any benefits being derived from his passing. So he decided to do an autopsy on Jacob's tree. Early on the next Saturday he gathered his tools and headed up to the mountain. He almost felt foolish performing an autopsy on a tree, but when he thought of how long that tree had lived and what stories it could tell if it had a voice, he made a firm resolve to precede the expedition no matter how long it took. He made arrangements with his boss to take an early holiday explaining that the wanted to do some thinking on personal matters while he hiked in the mountains.

Tony drove his jeep as close to the top of the mountain as he could. Then he unloaded his pack and gear. He put it on and hiked the remaining seven miles on foot. The carnage of the clear-cut made him want to weep. It seemed so foolish to strip the land bare. He knew the logic was that the edge effect would make the forest prosper. But edge effect or no edge effect, as far as he was concerned, nothing could replace the beauty of those tall trees, which had taken so many generations to grow.

After about six hours of hard hiking Tony had made his way to the base of the mountain. The last few hundred yards were, as it seemed, almost completely impassable. He marveled at how those dumb lumbermen could have possibly thought that they were going to get the tree out of here after they had cut it. When he reached the ledge on which Jacob had grown, he almost cried to think anyone would kill such a magnificent tree. He stood, looking down upon its shattered body thinking out loud "what a waste". Now it lay, a shattered hulk broken on the stones utterly defiled.

Tony set up camp at the base of the ledge and began his autopsy. He took his small chain saw out of his pack and cut the stump smooth so he could observe the rings. He found that Jacob's tree had its beginning 2,314 years ago. How very sad, thought Tony, imagine a tree that old. Why, that was born before the birth of Christ. He could see that when the tree had first taken root that the rains were much more regular than they are now, because the first 25 or 30 rings were wide and spaced far apart. Then along about 300 B.C. the climate began to change. Over a period of the next 15 years the rings got smaller and smaller. Until in 251 BC there was a major drought, which lasted until 247 BC. After that the tree began to grow again, slowly at first, then apparently in 236 BC the climate returned to normal again, producing 19 very large rings in succession.

It was not long into the work when Tony could see that this was going to be a much larger task than he originally had anticipated. He had not been up to the tree while it was alive and now that he was here it was apparent that the tree was much bigger than he originally thought. Because he was a flat-lander his head was spinning from lack of oxygen and he had severe headaches in those high altitudes. But what amazed him was how incredibly large this tree was. He had seen it only at a distance, which had caused him to grossly under estimated its size. Its trunk, though broken into a dozen pieces and shattered. Taking into account the placement of the pieces he measured it at just slightly over 138 feet long. The main branches were nearly 11 feet diameter and the trunk was just about 25 feet in diameter at the base. Jacob's tree was small by the Sequoia standards but so far as oaks go it was the largest one of its kind that he had ever seen. It certainly must have been a majestic tree when it was alive, Tony thought.

In 105 BC the top of the tree had been clipped off, possibly by an earthquake destroying the leading growth edge again. The remaining two topmost branch tips took over the growth, causing the tree to fork about halfway up the tree. It was amazing to Tony that a situation that occurred so long ago could so dramatically affect the tree. As Tony continued his investigation, he found a large scar about midway down the tree. He could see that about One A. D. a very heavy snowstorm had torn three of its larger branches from its trunk. The large gapping holes were filled over time with pitch and had no rings. The next three or four years showed thwarted growth, most likely due to the shock of losing so much of its foliage when the branches broke away. Jacob's tree must have come very close to dying then. But he managed to survive. For the next 29 year he grew taller and stronger. Each successive year the rings became darker and broader as the tree spread its roots and found new nourishment among the fractured rock.

Then about 32 or 33 AD Jacob's tree suffered a short and almost lethal drought. The rings for the next three years were very tight and almost indistinguishable because of their closeness and homogenous color. It occurred to Tony that of all of nature must have known of the Master's death. It seemed that Jacob's tree was mourning, refusing to grow.

During 200 AD Jacob's tree was under attack by blights and insects. His growth was erratic and thwarted; much as the young church struggled against the persecution of Rome in Asia and Europe so did Jacob struggle against the pestilence and disease. Ultimately both survived and grew to greater strength.

Jacob's tree was burned in a great fire which savagely scarred its northern branches and bark in 550 AD. But his strength endured and new growth rings showed the prosperity resulting from the clear burning of the vegetation around it, which reduced the competition for sparse but rich soil and sunlight.

During the War of the Roses, Jacob's tree experienced the first marks of man. Apparently someone cut a blaze mark at about what would have been five feet above the ground to mark a path. Perhaps some pre-Colombian Indian marked the tree to find his way back from a long hunting trip. Or a raiding band had marked him as a way of indicating the extent of their range. We may never know, but the blaze left a deep scar in the trunk, which filled with amber pitch. Over the years the pitch had hardened and was covered over by the healing process of the bark. It looked like a translucent amber jewel as it shined in the sun. How wonderful that this tree could make something of such beauty out of an unthinking attacks by a passer by.

In 1400 AD Jacob's tree suffered again from snow damage and a savage winter, which killed nearly one-fourth of its growth. But because part of the tree was willing to die, the remaining portion was allowed to live, and so Jacob survived. About 1490, when the New World was just being discovered, the Indians of the West were beginning to assert themselves again on the inner mountains of the Sierra Madre mountain range. Tony found four broken arrow points imbedded deeply in the skin of the tree at various heights. There was a lance point and several marks indicating that other arrow points had pierced his bark as well but had been removed. Judging from their location and the marks left at their entry into the tree, just as Columbus was setting the Spanish flag in the Caribbean soil, the Western Pawnee Indians were moving into these mountains. Evidently a group of native Mariposa Indians made a stand near the tree. We do know how this battle ended, but we do know that the Pawnee eventually eclipsed the Mariposa as the dominant tribe and the Mariposa faded into history.

Between then and the early 1800's Jacob's tree enjoyed rich rains and mild winters. Its growth rings were large and dark. In 1840 some trappers camped near the tree. They evidently made use of the late evenings boredom to shoot at a large knot in Jacob's tree. Tony found several pieces of musket lead and a mini ball imbedded in its wood. None of them were able to hit their mark so it was easy to see that they must have been drunk that night. After all, no mountain man would last long in the woods with marksmanship that poor.

Jacob's tree suffered and insect blight in 1855 and again in 1863. He was scarred by fire in 1868 and beetles attacked in 1882, 1890, 1893 and in 1898. But Jacob's tree survived, always-yielding a small bit of its growth in order to allow the rest of the tree to live and to prosper. Jacob's tree lived almost without blemish through the rest of the century and well into the next. And now in December of 1999 his life was ended. Not much was ever said by anyone in those parts about Jacobs Tree after it had been cut. After all everyone in the tiny town of Meridian knew how much they needed the prosperity that the lumberjacks brought. The town was poor and the infusion of cash from all those workers paychecks might make the difference in the survival or extinction of the town.

Yet when that tree died, something also died in the town. It just doesn't seem the same the old timers would say. No one could exactly put a finger on what was wrong, but I just did not seem the same without old Jacobs Tree on the top of the mountain. Tony never told anyone about dissecting the tree. I guess he thought they would laugh at him. But perhaps he more than anyone else in Meridian knew what was missing and that is why Meridian would never again be the same.

DAY OF THE LION

Martin Coleman was considered by everyone who knew him to be a loner. It wasn't really a fair thing to say. He tried many times to make friends, but he was never very good at it. He was shy, that is true, but also he was very gifted and much more intelligent than most of the people he went to school with. He would really get mad whenever anyone would tease him. He was an orphan who lived with his crotchety old aunt. He missed his mother and father whom had been killed in an unfortunate automobile accident some three years earlier. It had not been easy for him moving from the big city of Denver to this small town, but as he was still a minor, he had little choice. He used to say; "I guess I should consider myself lucky that Aunt Lucy took me in." After all, those state schools were pretty mean. Aunt Lucy tried her best to love him and to show him the right way to live, but she had never been married and at 57 it was very hard for her to try to raise a fifteen-year-old boy with such great hurts in his life. She did the best that she could. He was always well dressed, well fed and she took him to church weekly. He grudgingly went, not seeing much hope that sort of stuff, after all God had shattered his life and made him an orphan. He was a very sad and angry young man. It seemed that little that Aunt Lucy did reached him. So she prayed for him and worked hard to do her best. Perhaps the best thing that she did for him was to give him an old guitar she had gotten somewhere many years ago. She found it in the garage when she was doing the spring-cleaning and she thought if she could give him another outlet, maybe he would heal a bit faster. This was one of the few times that

Martins eyes lit up. When she took him to the garage and pulled the dusty case out from under a pile of nondescript boxes, his heart leapt.

When Martin opened the case, his eyes gleamed. It was a Martin, made in Segovia, Spain. He remarked, "Hey it has the same name as mine." Aunt Lucy knew that was not quite correct, but she smiled and nodded gently sensing that Martin was beginning to open up. It is beautiful he thought to himself. The body was rich Red Wood and the neck brilliant white Larch. Despite being consigned to the corner of the garage, the neck was still in good condition, although it needed a new bridge and strings. With a little WD40, the nuts worked flawlessly. He shined it, polished and oiled it until it gleamed. He had finally found a new friend. In time, that guitar became his best friend. He loved her, sang with and to her and he cared for her as though he had no other friends in the world.

It was very hard for Martin to adjust to small town life. Things were so different. There was no where to go, that is unless you counted the Bijou Theater where they changed the move once a month whether they needed to or not. He was a handsome young man. He had dark brown hair, hazel eyes and stood all of 4'-6" tall. He seemed to be a quiet person without much to offer, or so most people thought. But Martin was truly a gifted guitarist. He would spend his many long lonely hours with his guitar. He could make it sing and cry or even laugh. He loved his music and it seemed that his music and his guitar were his only friends. He would take her to his secret place in the forest and together they would escape the harshness of reality. The tenth grade was difficult for him, but somehow he managed to survive it. He wanted so much to be a part of the in crowd. No matter what he tried, it seemed as though nothing ever went right and everyone always ended up laughing at him. It did not take long for him to give up that idea. Again and again, he would retreat in shame to his special place in the forest.

Sattlersville, Georgia, where Martin lived wasn't much of a town. It had just slightly over 250 people. It was primarily a farming community. Nothing much ever happened there except the incessant gossip that kept the phone lines alive all hours of the day and night.

That is nothing except the circus. Well, it wasn't much of a circus. The Barnum and Barnum Circus was really not much more than a small carnival. It wasn't anywhere large enough to travel the main circuit, but it provided a tidy living for the clowns and jugglers who called it home. It came through almost every August, just as most of the people were about stir crazy with boredom and the stiff summer humidity.

The Barnum and Barnum Circus consisted of fourteen wagons, a dozen games, four rides, a dilapidated Ferris wheel, an old elephant and one Lion. The Lion's name was Samson and his rather untalented trainer taught him all of the common tricks. He could jump through a burning hoop, ride a barrel and roll over like a trained dog. Samson was a young lion who had been raised all his life in captivity. He knew nothing about hunting, because Max his trainer always took care of him. Samson was a magnificent animal, just over three and one-half years old. The circus was very proud of him; the ringmaster would always introduce the act with great flourish. They thought of it as quite an act, though by most standards it was poor. But it was the most exciting the circus had to offer, and it was a good draw bringing in a goodly sum every time they set up the big top.

Martin really enjoyed the fun and excitement of the circus. Like everyone in town, he was a big kid at heart and was just dying to see something, anything to break the monotony of the long boring hot summer days. That first night, he decided not to go. He knew that the gang would be sure to go and they would delight in the opportunity to pick on him. Also, it just didn't seem right to go alone. He wanted to take a date and just could not get one. It seemed that no one wanted him around. They were embarrassed to have him with them. He was very hurt by all of this, although he never told anyone. It made him want to cry, but he could not. He had not wept sense the funeral of his parents. No matter how much he wanted to weep he just could not do it.

That first night he went to his special meadow in the forest where he sat alone and sang his songs as he always did. As he sat there singing, he the words of his songs wept for his loneliness. When he stopped to rest his fingers, he wondered aloud, "Why has God had allowed me to be so sad and to have to live like this?" He pondered the question for a few moments as he looked up into the deep black sky studded with brilliant stars. After a while, a cool breeze began to blow and he soon fell into a restless sleep when he had a vision.

The Master said, "Martin my child, I know all of your hurts, and your sadness. I too have been mocked and rejected. I remember well these things during the days of my trials. I also remember the tears, which I bore for you. I love you son and I do not want you to suffer. Have hope now Martin, your life seems so bleak and so meaningless, but know my child, that I have chosen you to do my special work. I have cultivated your life. Know that your days of aloneness here are almost over. Have courage and strength for a mighty test will come, and when it has passed all those who called you fool will be a feeble compared to you."

With that said, the radiant vision vanished and Martin awoke trembling. He could hardly believe what had just happened. He was excited and thrilled beyond measure. He wanted to jump so high as to touch the clouds. He was so happy. He grabbed his guitar and ran rapidly toward the town with excitement. By the time that he got to the outskirts of the town, reason had caught up with him. He thought to himself, man that was a foolish dream. I can't tell anyone about that dream they will think that I am crazy. So Martin brushed the dream from his mind and went home for the night.

Early the next afternoon, he arrived to the sounds of commotion. The entire town was alive with excitement as the circus was going to do a second unplanned show. Martin was also excited, but not for the same reason. He was excited because he had the same dream again that night, except this time the Master had told him that today all of this was going to happen. Martin couldn't believe it, and still, he couldn't tell anyone it just seemed too crazy. So, he grabbed his guitar, pillow, and a blanket and made for the circus. Maybe he could forget this nonsense and have some fun for a while, he thought.

When he got to the circus, it seemed that the entire town, as well as the entire county had already arrived. It was filled with hundreds of people. The smell of cotton candy was in the air and it made his mouth water. The barkers filled the air with great voices hawking their wares and the wonderful confusion excited him even more. He knew that it was going to be a fun day, one of the few fun days that he was going to have that summer. His eyes bulged with excitement when he rushed up to the first refreshment booth and saw the program. With his guitar dangling on his shoulder, he bought a ticket and made for the big top. He bought himself a large cone of cotton candy, a caramel apple and an extra large soft drink. Gulping the drink and eating the cotton candy as he walked, he moved out into the crowd toward the tent.

Unknown to him, at the time some, of his schoolmates were standing nearby watching. Stanley Grossenback, the class bully, poked Fred Crowder in the side saying, "Watch this." With that, he snuck up behind Martin and stuck his foot out into his path between Martin's legs. Because Martin was so involved in his cotton candy, he did not see the foot and he fell forward spilling everything in his hands as he fell flat on his face. An explosion of laughter immediately surrounded him, as his schoolmates roared at the spectacle. Within a few minutes, everyone around him in the crowd had joined in the fun. "Look at the Klutz!" they were saying. Martin froze for a moment in absolute terror, then picked up his candy covered guitar and soda and ran in embarrassment through the crowd. He shoved people out of his way and made his way into the forest weeping uncontrollably. Fortunately for him, his guitar had not been damaged by the prank, but it would have to be re-tuned. When he got to his special place, he sat down crying until he had no more tears. After some time, he gathered his composure and began to clean his guitar. He took out his handkerchief and tenderly wiped her bridge clean. He lovingly wiped the soda water off her face and cleaned her sticky neck. He held her close, as though she was a hurt child. He stroked her, as she was his girl friend and began to weep all over again when he noticed a large scratch on her side. After a time he began to strum her sadly. He slowly played as he prayed.

When the laughter died down around the refreshment stand, most of the people went back to what they were doing. That is, everyone but Stanley and Fred. They were still looking for more excitement, when they walked past the lion's cage. Samson was asleep in the cage with his back pressed tight against the bars. Stanley snickered and poked Fred again and reached for a nearby stick. Silently creeping up behind Samson, he reared back and jabbed him, with the sharp end of the stick. Samson bolted to his feet with a loud roar, wheeled around and swatted furiously at his unseen enemy with a swift swing of his right paw. Frightened, Stanley jumped back a few steps, knocking Fred over as the cage swayed under the full force of the 285-pound angry cat. Our brave heroes loved it, so they began to alternately taunt the cat. They made loud noises and danced back and forth, causing the cat to quickly move its head from left to right and back again. Fred used the stick to bang between the bars, making a loud metallic noise, while his buddy picked up a hand full of pebbles and periodically threw them at Samson.

Egged on by the cat's response, Stanley ran the stick back and forth across the bars of the cage faster and faster. The stick made a louder and louder clanking sound, inciting Samson to even greater anger. Fred joined in with a second stick on the opposite side of the cage. They both reviled as Samson turned this way and that to meet his tormentor's attack. In the frenzy of growling and clangs, Stanley unwittingly loosened the latch of the cage with one swing of the stick. Just as Samson's trainer Max arrived to subdue the boys. Samson lunged at the cage one more time and the door sprung open. The trainer heard the clank of the latch falling open and turned just in time to see Samson spring through the air toward him. He covered his face with his arms and braced for the attack. Samson was frantic, he ran over his trainer as though he was not even standing there, leaving him face down in the dust but unhurt.

Both of the boys ran in opposite directions away from the fleeing cat screaming at the top of their voices that the lion had gotten loose. Instant panic broke out in the circus, as hundreds of spectators stampeded away in every direction in terror. In the confusion of screams, falling stands, and breaking wood, Samson panicked even more. All he could do was to instinctively run for the safety of the forest. Samson was even more confused and afraid than the people were. He had never known freedom. He had never been out of his cage, for more than a few minutes at a time before, during and after his show. He had been raised in captivity from a cub. The noise and commotion made him want to run. Instinctively that is what he did. He charged forward running over Stanley, as he was fleeing in terror. Samson knocked him over like a bowling pin, knocking him unconscious, and disappeared into the under brush.

Fourteen people were hurt that day in the panic, plus Stanley who had large scratch marks down his back and the trainer who was knocked unconscious by the weight of the cat brushing him aside. But, fortunately no one was killed. That was a miracle, considering the number of people involved and the panicked stampede. Fortunately the center pole of the big top stood the shattering force of everyone pushing under the tents edge. It did not fall but the side flaps of the tent were damaged beyond repair.

Within the hour, the County Sheriff summoned a citizens armed posse. They formed up in the parking lot next to the big top to track down the dangerous lion that had savagely mauled three people (two of whom coincidentally neglected to mention that they were tormenting the beast). By the time they formed up, it was nearly dark. Sheriff Heard gave explicit instructions that no one was to shoot at the cat unless they were attacked, afraid they might wound it in the night and a wounded cat would be ten times more dangerous to deal with. The posse was armed with all manors of weapons. Everything from deer rifles to shotguns, revolvers to an old WW II bayonet, and one man even had a saber, although no one was sure that he had any idea what to do with it should he need it. They were sent out in groups of three with instructions to stick together and to carefully search an assigned area in the hope of surrounding the cat before he got too deep into the forest.

By now Martin, had fallen asleep in the forest. He was wakened by the sounds of sporadic gunfire as the nervous stalker shot at everything that moved. Martin recognized the sound of rifle fire and became nervous. He thought about going home, but he wasn't quite ready for that yet. So he picked up his guitar and began to softly strum her. He quietly played "Lay Your Hands On Me" more to calm himself than anything else. As he sat there humming and gently strumming, Samson (who was nearby hiding under a fallen log near a large oak tree) perked up his ears. By this time he had calmed and he was made curious by the music. So he crawled out from under the log tree and moved cautiously through the underbrush. Just as Samson came to the edge of the small meadow that Martin was in, he stepped on a twig. The cracking sound caused Martin to look up from his guitar straight into the eyes of the trembling lion only some ten feet away.

They both froze petrified at the sight of each other. Samson began to swish his tail nervously and crouched slightly as if to pounce. Martin's heart pounded wildly as the lion fidgeted slowly back and forth then got up and sat down next to the log that Martin had been seated against. They both just sat there looking at each other for a moment. Then, Martin remembered what the vision had told him, the night before. He slowly moved to pick up his guitar. Martin began to strum Rev. Landry's song again as Samson cautiously moved another step closer to him, pausing with his fore paw raised, swishing his tail nervously. Martin began to sing, nervously at first but then with greater courage . . . "Lay your hand gently upon us, lay your hand upon our heads, let their touch render you peace, let them bring you forgiveness and healing, lay your hands gently, lay your hands." . . . .

The sound of his singing got the attention of two members of the posse, who were within earshot. They came into the meadow a few minutes later up wind of Samson, just as the cat began to walk slowly toward Martin. One man raised his rifle to shoot, but the second stopped him because it was impossible to hit the cat from where they were without also hitting Martin. They watched in amazement while Samson walked up to Martin's feet and lay down. As Martin continued to sing, Samson turned over on his side and purred, pawing the grass playfully. Martin kicked off one of his penny loafers and began to scratch Samson behind the left ear with his big toe as he continued to play. Samson closed his eyes contented and started to fall asleep.

At that moment, James the third member of the posse team arrived in the meadow, bursting through the brush like a wild elephant. Samson sprang to his feet and began swishing his tall wildly, growling while shifting his head to the left and right in an effort to locate the disturbance. Martin got up quietly, as Samson began to growl. James froze, panic stricken as Samson took two tenuous steps towards him and then stopped. Martin cleared his throat and then with great authority said, "Samson lay down." Samson turned his head toward Martin and then obediently sat down. Martin walked up to Samson and kneeling next to him, began to scratch his ear with his hand, to everyone's amazement. Samson turned his head into the scratch, enjoying every moment of it. This continued as five other posse members arrived. They all stood staring in amazement at what they were witnessing.

Martin rose to his feet and motioned to everyone to stay absolutely still. He was going to take Samson back to his cage. Sheriff Heard obediently motioned with his hands for everyone to put down their weapons and remain quiet. Martin and Samson turned slowly back toward the circus. Martin placed his hand on Samson's mane and sang as he led him, "Lay your hands and gently upon us . . . When they got to his cage, Martin opened the door and Samson obligingly jumped in. The moment the door clanged shut a tremendous roar went up from the trackers who had followed him at a distance. Samson let out a mighty roar in discontentment at the abrupt noise. Martin was the hero of the day. Everyone was excited and happy that the danger was over. When the cheers died down, Sheriff Heard asked Martin how he did it. Martin said, "I prayed and I played my guitar." Clearly this is the story of a common boy with an uncommon faith. From the day after none of the old gang messed with him again.

HANDS OF THE MASTER

F rank Zeni is an honorable and just man. He was known throughout the city for his kindness and his generosity. He was especially fond of children and delighted in giving them candy. His life had been full and there were many good memories in his heart to sustain him in these golden years of his life. His life had been full and he knew that he had no reason to complain because he had lived a very good life. He had gone to college, experienced a fulfilling career as an architect and had met a woman whom he loved greatly. She had become his wife and borne him two fine sons and two daughters. Now that Frank was 88, he knew that soon it would be his time to return to the master.

As he sat at the back of the auction room, he dozed in a restless sleep. These last few years had not been kind to him. His failing body had spent his life's savings and now he was forced to sell all his possessions in order to pay his medical bills. He had not always saved, as he should. Investing was always too scary for him and he really never thought about his retirement. Although his life as an architect was aesthetically fulfilling, often the only fringe benefit to his work (other than aesthetic satisfaction) was his monthly paycheck and then not every month at that. After paying the staff, personnel expenses and home bills there was rarely anything left over to save for retirement.

Frank was a proud man and refused to ask for anyone's help. He had always made his own way in the world and at 88 he wasn't about to change. Besides, he would say, John and Alfred, his sons, had their problems. Samantha, his daughter was pregnant with her second child.

To ask her help would certainly deprive her child, so he refused to do that. Anna was not yet finished with university study and she could ill afford any help. He refused even to tell his children that he was broke or holding this auction.

As Frank dozed, the auctioneer began the proceedings. Every book of his carefully collected library, all of his furniture gathered over a lifetime of travel, his small eclectic house, and even his old 1939 Oldsmobile Rocket 88 was to go up on the auction block. Frank slept through most of the proceedings, oblivious to what was going on. His possessions meant little to him. He measured his wealth by his children and the rich trove of memories gathered over seven continents and many thousands of miles of world travel.

As he slept, he conjured up wonderful memories of by gone years. He smiled as he remembered the first time that he held his sons. What a wonder he thought, a small thing such as a child is. How wonderful that we, Helen and I, have created this. A warm pleasure filled his whole body again as he relived that moment. He remembered how after returning from the hospital that day, he went into the study as he had done so many times before, picked up his viola and played out the joy of the moment. He expressed in music what he could not say in words. He remembered the many many times that he played his viola; singing out in notes the depthless feelings that he felt in his heart (but could not speak). He also remembered the many times he had played his children to sleep that the viola. It was just as much a part of the family as they were. These were rich moments replete with love and affection. He also remembered hearing a story much like the one that he was living right now that was told by his pastor in a long ago sermon. But his love of his viola, his children and the sweet music the viola made when he played her filled his heart with enormous satisfaction. This made him both happy and sad.

He remembered the day that the American Institute of Architects bestowed their highest honor, the AIA Fellow, upon him. How wonderful it felt to receive the recognition of his peers. He was now truly a master, a master architect. He went into the study and played for almost three hours in thanks and joy for that day. The viola was almost an alternative part of his ego. It could sing when he could not.

He loved her almost as much as he did his profession or his house, that is if one could love an object (as he was accustom to say!)

When John and Alfred got married, he proudly played the wedding march for them with a mastery that few people had ever heard before. Again, when their children were born, he played the viola, rejoicing and offering thanksgiving to the master for his goodness. That viola was an extension of Frank. It was just as natural a part of him as were his arms. The bow, which he used with such mastery to make his viola sing, or weep, or laugh for joy, was little more than an extension of his hands when he played. Many suggested that he could have easily made a better living as a concert violist. But he would always blush and remind him that architecture was his chosen profession. After all, he had struggled to five years of bachelors work, two years of master's study, a two-part one-year professional examination and two years internship before he could hang out his shingle. He was an architect and he was delighted to be so.

That somber day two years ago when the one great love of his life, his Helen died, he played his beloved viola, washing it in tears. He remembered after everyone else had left the grave, he stood there to the wee hours of the morning, and played a farewell to his beloved Helen. It was such a sad melody, but it was from the heart and full of life. The viola seemed to weep with him and shared his burden. Together they found solace in a very deep moment of sadness.

So much of life had transpired between, in and around the instrument and him, he affectionately called her Bless. It was she of all his possessions that he was most reluctant to part with, even though his arthritis would no longer permit him to played her very well. Not sense Helen had died had he played his beloved Bless. It was much too painful. Not so much that it hurt his fingers, than it hurt his heart not to have Helen there to listen to his songs of love and fidelity. Now in the latter days of his life he looked sadly upon the remains of his possessions knowing that though he did not want to surrender all these wonderful things that he had gathered from across the world over so many years he knew that he had no choice. It must be done, they had to be sold. He had nothing left with which to continue to pay his bills.

As the gavel came down upon the stand particularly hard, Frank bolted awake. The auctioneer barked, what am I offered for this old viola. It's not a Stradivarius, but it can carry a fine tune. Two dollars, or three? Now ladies and gentlemen, it may be a bit scratched, and it does have a chip on the nut, but it will still play a beautiful song. Five dollars? Fifteen, I hear 20, 20 . . . 20! Going once . . . . Frank was shocked to hear what was happening to his Bless. As he got up and tottered toward the front of the room, he began to quietly weep. He turned toward the audience and with a strong gesture demanded Bless be given to him. Everyone stopped their murmuring and watched intently as this disheveled old man drew out the bow from the case. With an authoritative gesture he mounted the bow on the viola. He took a moment to tune it then placing it under his chin, began to play.

He began with the Avia Maria then he movement to the aria for Madame Butterfly and then into Paganini's flight of the bumblebee, and then Staint-Saens Symphony in C Minor. That old scratched viola sang like a nightingale. Everyone in the audience was mesmerized by the richness of the music. Its depth was enormous and it's timber incredible. When he finished, he handed the viola back to the auctioneer and returned to his seat at the back of the room.

Now ladies and gentlemen, what am I bid for this magnificent instrument? Frank smiled broadly as someone up front barked 1,000 dollars, then two, three, three five, 5,000 dollars. Soon there after he sat down, he closed his eyes and passed from this world into the next, knowing that the money would be well spent by the Depelchen Orphanage to whom he had willed it. No one seemed to notice thinking that he had gone back to sleep.

As the room cleared and the successful bidder carried his prize out the door, a young man of 18 standing in the back of the audience watching the auction, approached the auctioneer and asked, "Sir, what changed? Why was so much money paid for that beat up old scratched viola? It is the same one we saw before that old man played it. What made it so much more valuable?" Young man the auctioneer said, "It was touched by the hand of the Master, that is what gave it such value."

A-PAIR-OF-BULL

There once was a pair of bulls who were born in the same pasture on the same day in Galilee. Samuel was a strong brown bull and Jacob a good looking black bull with a white spot on his forehead. Both calves grew up under the tender care of their mothers and both were suckled with rich milk that was abundant with the fatness of the land. Samuel was a feisty young bull, who enjoyed charging the other calves and making mock battle. He was strong, handsome and everyone said he was very special. His mother was very proud of him because he was so aggressive, after all he had come from a long line of strong bulls that brought much honor to their owners. She constantly preened him, licking his hair and being sure that he was always in prime view of the attendants. She was very proud of him and wanted to be sure that the cattle handlers could see what a find young bull he was.

Jacob was timid. Whenever Samuel would challenge him, he would back down and constantly suffer the sarcastic mocking of his peers. His mother could not understand why he was so afraid. He too came from a strong lineage of good bulls. She would chastise him and try to shame him into the proper action. Regardless of how hard he tried, he could not be aggressive. It was just not in him. So, he was soon labeled a coward and everyone made fun of him at every opportunity. This shamed his mother, who in turn started to neglect him. Whenever the cattle handlers would gather the herd, she would always push him behind her so that no one could see how little and scruffy he was.

Over the next few months, Jacob would endure many insults because he just did not see any reason for fighting. It just didn't make any sense to him. Jacob was by his nature a very gentle calf and he did his best to be what he felt he should be. Despite this mocking, Jacob began to realize that perhaps there was a real mission for him in his life. So, whenever Samuel or the other calves would make fun of him he would walk off to the corner of the meadow to talk with God and ask for strength.

Some weeks later the landowner came into the meadow to survey his herd. Samuel's mother was so proud of him. She cleaned him and licked his hair down, she primped and preened him and together with much pomp and to-do, paraded in front of their Master. Jacob's mother was ashamed to have him seen. When her turn came to be shown to the owner, she hung her head and pushed Jacob behind her as they walked slowly down the path. Much to everyone's surprise, the Master stopped and demanded to see Jacob. Jacob, as surprised as the rest, threw back his head stood erect and walked as stately as he could in front of the owner. He could hear his peers laughing and snickering at him in the background, but it did not matter to him, he did his best. The laughing did not make any difference to him, because he knew he had a mission in life. God had told him so and he believed what he had been told.

At the end of the day, the ranch master had his herd separated for the upcoming spring sale. One fourth of the young calves were sold to a man in Jerusalem for market, half of them were returned to the valley and the rest were driven north with their mothers to the winter pasture. Samuel and Jacob were separated from their mothers and taken to the owner's house. There was much talk in the pasture that day about who had gone where and what had happened to whom. Samuel's mother was particularly pleased and she pranced back and forth gloating over the fact that her Samuel had been chosen to go to the Master's house. Jacob's mother was confused and bit her tongue wondering why Jacob also had been chosen. She made her way to the corral next to the Master's house, where she struck up a conversation with Saul, the Master's personal donkey. Of course, just as any mother would be, she was very concerned about her son. She was worried and wanted to know exactly where he was. With some coaxing, she persuaded Saul to tell her where they had been taken. She was shocked to hear that Samuel had been taken to the fattening pen. Also she was much relieved to find out that Jacob had been given to an inn-keeper in Bethlehem in payment of a debt.

When Samuel's mother heard of the plight of her son, she flew into a rage. How could they, why he is the best young bull in the herd. How could they, the fattening pen, to the fattening pen! Samuel had no idea of what was in store for him. He just knew that because he was so handsome and strong he was being given such wonderful treatment. He was given a double measure of maize and oats. He was given as much fresh silage as he could eat. Every second day there was molasses. There was always fresh green grass to eat and from time to time bits of old bread. He had a great deal of cold clear well water to drink and soon he put on 150 pounds.

The next June, a great commotion erupted around the farm. After many questions, it was discovered that the Master's son, who had run away to Damascus in rebellion, had come home. The Master had taken off his best robe, and his new shoes and given them to him. He had even given him his signet ring. Who had ever heard of such a thing, to do such a thing for such a rebellious child. There was to be a feast. Samuel didn't even understand what that meant, but his mother began her wail in lamentation for her son. He was butchered that day for the feast. While the people's rejoicing rang through the valley Samuel's mother wept for her foolish son who was so preoccupied with himself that he understood nothing of what was going to happen to him, even to the last moment when he was butchered.

Jacob's days were much leaner than Samuel's. He was relegated to the plow. He spent his days in hard toil beneath the hot sun. There was always plenty of straw to eat and water, even though it was hot and dirty, it was enough to meet his needs. Every once in a while his master would give him a few oats, but never more than a handful, after all they were quite expensive and the innkeeper just was not making enough money on the inn to buy them very often. Times were hard and the taxes of the Romans were very demanding. It was everything that all of the town's people could do to keep home and hearth together.

The next year a great cry went out throughout the region. Caesar Augustus had proclaimed that a census must he taken of the entire empire. All of Bethlehem was in a bustle. People were coming from all over. They came from Egypt from Caesura, from Phillipi, from Antioch, Minos, Alexandria, from all over the world to be registered. Caesar had declared that all men must return to the town of their birth for the census. The innkeeper was delighted, never had business been so good. Never had there been so many people in the town. Soon the inn was filled to capacity and not a room remained. People were even sleeping side by side on the floor of the dining room and in the halls.

Late that evening, another long departed son of the town, who had been born there some 30 years earlier, came to the inn and asked for a room. There as no place to put him, much less room his pregnant wife. He was directed to the stable behind the inn, where they could lay down and get out of the cold winter wind. Jacob was delighted to see them as they came up the hill. As the woman dismounted her donkey, he thought, how wonderful a woman with child. He quickly herded the sheep aside and made a pile of straw for her to lie on. She laid down her head at his feet and soon fell asleep.

In the course of the evening, her time came to give birth to her child. Her husband rushed out and returned shortly with a midwife. The midwife sent him off for water and rags. Jacob lay down at her head and did what he could to keep things quiet in the stable. The rooster and hens just simply couldn't sit still, or so it seemed. After a time, she gave birth to a son. Oh how beautiful he was, Jacob thought. The husband took off his robe and wrapped his son in it. While he was gently rocking the babe, Jacob got his feet and moved toward the manger to rearrange the hay. Picking up a mouthful of fresh straw from the back of the stable, he laid it in the manger.

By this time, some shepherds had come to the stable with wide eyes and began to tell excitedly a wild story about angels singing and of strange lights. The husband placed his little son in the freshly matted hay, and went to attend his wife. Jacob thought to himself, what a wonderful beautiful baby this is. He seems so strong and so peaceful. What can I do to help, he thought, I'm only a dumb old bull, what can I do? He hesitated a moment. Then an idea hit him. I can warm him with my breath. The night was cold and the child had begun to shiver. How wonderful it was for me to be here, Jacob thought, with this little child and I can help him by keeping him warm with my breath.

Jacob stood there all night warming the child while Joseph and Mary slept. Just as the sun came, up three richly dressed men came to the stable. One spoke to Joseph, then he laid a chest at the foot of the manger. His two companions did the same thing, and then sat down and talked of following a great star, which had led them to a new king. Asking himself, Jacob said, "A new king, Jacob thought, a king, I've been attending a king!!!" Oh how exciting I've warmed the new king. Oh how wonderful our God is. He has let me attend a newborn king. He has not failed me, I've been given a great charge, and a wonderful mission and I'm so happy, me a lowly bull, what an honor.

The next day, the three men, Mary, Joseph and the baby left Bethlehem to continue their journeys in different directions. Jacob could hardly believe it had happened. He couldn't believe that God would choose him to care for the new king. This was the experience that God had promised him. Jacob lived many years thereafter and died a natural death at a ripe old age. Wherever he went he told of that cold night when he attended the new King of Israel. He told of Mary, her husband and the three rich men and how he warmed the baby with his breath.

JOHN FRANK

John Frank was born into a coal mining family in Upper Heyford, England in 1839. His father was a hard-working man who worked himself into an early grave providing for his family. He was a good man, who dearly loved his family. Although he did not like the coalmines, it was all that he had ever known and everyone in his family had always been a coal miner. It was hard work, but it was honest. He worked very hard to provide for his large family.

But John, unlike his three older brothers, decided at an early age that mining coal and the Black Death were not the things he wanted from life. Early in his life, he found an affinity for the forest. He could always be found wandering through the woods near his home or in one of the nearby fields. On a number of occasions, he was caught by the landowners who looked unkindly upon commoners in THEIR forest. He suffered several beatings and two chastisements at the end of double OTT buckshot in very short order. After all a commoner was always thought to be a poacher when caught in the woodlands belonging to the gentry. He was really lucky, as he might have been hung for such an offense had they chosen to pursue the matter. This of course concerned his parents, as they did not want to see him hurt. John's parents first noticed his love of wood and they encouraged him to carve, but only as a hobby. After all, one could not make a living at such a craft, or so they thought.

When it came time for him to choose a profession and to take a job, he chose woodworking. He loved the trees and the smell of fresh swan wood. To be able to work in the presence of their effervescent smell thrilled him to his core. John had always wanted to learn how to carve in wood, yet he was practical and he knew that it was difficult to make a living as an artist, so he decided on the construction trade.

His first job was with the White Star Shipyard in Portsmouth. He worked hard at his apprenticeship and quickly became a journeyman. With the attainment of his new status, came more money and the natural cycle of youth began to follow. He was away from home and family. He was lonely and being the low man on the totem pole, so to speak, he was always the brunt of jokes. Also being of small stature only added to the assaults by his fellow workers. So over time, more out of sadness and loneness, he started to drink. Before he knew it, he had spent the next few years in drinking and riotous living. His face was a well-established fixture at the local pub. He was always the first to come and the last to leave, and never sober.

Then in 1860 John met Lillian O'Leary. She had been the most sought after young lady in all of Portsmouth's working class. They met quite by accident, as she stumbled on a street curb and fell into John's arms when he was passing on the sidewalk. She spilled her packages all over him and the street. John was a small, slender man with soft blue eyes, light brown hair and a powerful jaw. Immediately, Lillian was attracted to him. His strong hands particularly impressed her, as he caught her in the fall. Lillian's gentle white skin brushed Johns and he was enthralled by the gentle smell of the lilacs she wore in her hair. As he reached out to break her fall, her heart pounded at the strength of his rich bronze arms. His eyes watered at the delicate beauty of her eyes and the curve of her face.

Lillian was a good woman of 17 who had been fortunate to be an only child born into a middle-class merchant family. Her father spoiled her with the finest clothing and the best of perfume, which she wore with grand elegance and style. Lillian was a very special woman. She did not seek the rich or the powerful men of her day, all of who flocked around her. She would have been a great prize to any of them who might convince her to become theirs. Rather she spurned their affections. She knew that love born of heated passion would soon pass away and that a marriage of status would be doomed to sadness. She also understood that love born of economic convenience would be a sham at best. Despite that being the custom of the day, she resisted her father's attempts at match making. What she sought was a love born of a good spirit that would endure the tests of time.

Over time, Lillian became interested in John, as they would pass every day or so on the sidewalk. Lillian mused how silly it seemed that she would be attracted to such a drunkard and a braggart. Yet she had felt a great attraction to this man John. She sensed there was much more to this fellow than initially met the eye. John, for his part, felt that she was far above his station and he made no advances. He thought her to be utterly unattainable, far too beautiful to ever be interested in someone like him. But after several flirting passes on the sidewalk, he began to hope otherwise.

Lillian was fortunate to be from a strong church going family. Her father and her mother were both vitally interested in her spiritual as well as physical growth. They taught her well and every night before dinner they would start the meal with ample readings from the Family Bible. As she grew into womanhood, she came into a strong relationship with God. Somehow, it seemed that He was whispering in her ear to prepare herself for John. She was a bit shy and confused about that message. She was also hopeful, excited and at the same time afraid. He was both beautiful and dangerous. He was handsome and unruly. He excited her and he made her cautious at the same time. She reluctantly decided to try to meet him more formally (as was the custom of the day.)

She made a rather obvious stumble into him again as they passed on the sidewalk the following Saturday. Lillian feinted a sprained ankle in order to get John to take her home and when they got there she invited him to come in for tea. They both had a riotous time laughing at their second "chanced" meeting and the grand spectacle they made of themselves picking up all Lillian's packages twice after bumping again into each other in the process. After tea, Lillian showed John the door and they, much to her embarrassment, laughed again at her miraculous healing. They both agreed to meet the next Tuesday for more tea.

John's heart pounded uncontrollably. How could he be so lucky? What had happened that he should be able to find such a fine women who was actually interested in him. He made a firm resolve to straighten up and stop drinking. He knew that he must if he was to continue to see such a wonderful women. After a proper courtship, the obligatory asking of her hand from her father (and his reluctant acquiescence) in May of that year they were married in the courtyard of Plymouth Cathedral among the magnificent oaks which grew there. Somehow, to John it seemed so right that they should be joined in this small forest, because his love of wood was now complemented by his love for his new wife.

Those first few years were difficult because John had not made full progress in breaking his old drinking habits. Yet their love was rich and deep for each other. John would carve little figurines of deer and sheep for her and she would always cook him a sumptuous meal after each day's work. Together they worked hard for his healing and in time it flowered full. In time, John came to understand the richness of God's love and his desire to drink and carouse faded. Because of Lillian's love he had grown to know God's richness and their relationship was magnified tenfold. For the first time in many many years he had great peace.

John had hoped that one day Lillian would give them children, but sadly she was barren and unable to have children. John was greatly saddened by this yet undaunted. His love of God had grown so great that he was willing to believe in the impossible. Though he, in his worldly wisdom did not expect his wife to become miraculously pregnant, he was not expecting to receive children quite in the manner in which he received them. Because his love was full and rich he accepted the gift when it came. When he found two orphaned brothers weeping on his doorstep, he gladly welcomed them into his home as his own.

Jimmy was eight and Joseph six. As dirty and scruffy as they were, they were quickly cleaned up and welcomed home. John enjoyed carving small toys for them. The boys quickly became the greatest delights of John and Lillian's hearts. Both boys grew rapidly in strength and maturity. Although the boys had some difficult times, John was always there to help them work things out. With the great wealth of

love that John had and his gift of carving, he was always able to make
the boys smile and quickly forget their little traumas.

In 1893 John made the momentous decision to move to America.
Work had been difficult to find in England because of the Industrial
Revolution had destroyed his trade. No one wanted to employ a
shipwright. After all, wooden ships were obsolete. Wood had given way
to iron and then soon to steel. No longer was John able to provide for
his wife and children in Portsmouth, which had long been his home.
His hope was that he might find work, repairing fishing boats for
the New England fishermen. So, he immigrated to America with the
intent of sending for his family when he could make enough money
for passage. Besides, his boys were big enough to earn enough money
to provide for themselves and Lillian.

When he got to America, he was very surprised. The few jobs there
were available were jealously guarded from the incursions of foreigners
such as he. He could find little work in wood. He first tried to work
making barrels. But that did not last long. He simply could not break
the tight control of guilds, which controlled the wood working craft in
the area. They just did not want any foreign competition. Ultimately,
he found himself sweeping floors in a saloon. Over the next few
months, he fell into despair and loneliness, which led him back to
drinking. It was only a few months later; he got fired for missing work
one time to many, hung over. It was not long before the word was out.
He was a drunkard. He could find no work anywhere.

So, John resorted to riding the rails, the life of a hobo, from
one camp to the next and doing odd jobs whenever they came
along. Despite his difficulties, he retained his indomitable love of
woodworking, even to the point of carving figurines to give to the
street children. In the summer of 1894, John found himself in Houston
where he hoped to find work. Actually he hadn't planned to stay in
Houston except he fell off the train while sleeping on the rail under
a cattle car when it took an unexpected lurch while linking up to
another car. Fortunately, he landed in a thicket, which broke his fall.
He was scratched, but unhurt.

Houston was a boomtown in that day. Like a wide-eyed boy, he
gawked at the bigness of the city. There seemed to be such a wonderful

bustle to Houston. So much activity, such a noise, he thought. Perhaps I can find work in wood here. He spent the first night at the Star of Hope Mission on Crawford Street, sharing his bunk with another hobo. It was a bit smelly, but at least it was out of the weather. After a hearty breakfast of bread and bean soup, it was off to the construction sites to find work. The first site that he tried the foreman took one look at him and wouldn't even speak to him (he was too old). Thereafter, it was the same old story, you're too old. You'll get hurt. Or you'll just be in the way. John was dejected, but determined. For most of the rest of the week he strove earnestly to find work, but was always turned away.

Finally he came to Michael J. Clines, foreman for the construction of the New Esperson Building. Michael was a burly man of 6'-4" who had been in construction most of his life. He knew the field very well. He well understood the taxing nature of his work. But, Michael's heart was as big as he was. When John asked for work, he simply could not turn away his pleading eyes. "What ya do?" Michael barked. "Why, I'm a wood-wright. I . . . I carve in wood. Uh, here," John said, thrusting an intricately carved piece of wood into Michael's hand. Michael looked at the three dancing bears no more than two inches tall holding hands and carved out of one piece of red oak.

"My," he said, "these are wonderful. They're so small, yet I can see their eyes and the hair on their arms. My, my, look at that! We don't have much call for wood carving but I'll tell you what I'll do," he said. "You can carve the ceiling in the entry, okay? I'll give you $10 a week, take it or leave it." Of course John took the offer! That was a very good wage in that day. John would spend little and sent most of it back to his family in Europe.

He reported with his tools promptly at 5:30 a.m. the next morning for work. For the next seven-and-a-half months, John would climb the scaffolding in the main lobby and carve on the ceiling. The horrible clanging and pounding of the riveting did not seem to bother him much. Really, no one even knew he was there. He would always work late and never missed a day. Michael almost forgot that he had hired him. That is until late in the following February, when he did not show up for his monthly payday. Michael was a very busy man and he barely noticed until he counted his check stubs at the end of the day. He looked carefully through the Payroll Signature book and found that John's signature was missing.

Michael thought that perhaps John had fallen asleep or something. As he walked to the building from the construction shack, he heard a loud crash come from inside the building. Rushing quickly up to the front door he saw John's tools scattered all over the floor. He quickly ran up the gangplank and sprang to the top of the scaffolding. There he found John face down in a pile of shavings. Michael stooped over to feel John's pulse. There wasn't any. It was evident that John had suffered a heart attack. Michael picked him up, brushed the sawdust from his face and out of his white beard, to reveal a gentle smile rather than the face cringing with pain.

As he lifted his flashlight and shined it around him, he could see the magnificence of John's work. Every beam and column top was intricately carved with dental and oak leaf clusters. There were hundreds of angels and cherubs. A common arch had been transformed into a magnificent multi-foil arch and he had carved a net tracery above the main window. Half-a-dozen parapets surrounded the room in ordered symmetry. Nebule molding adorned the edges of the room. The flat portions of the ceiling were woven with inlaid sectileonus of various shades of wood. The whole room was a magnificent array of detailed woodwork never before seen by anyone in this part of the country. Each piece was hand-rubbed and seemed to glow with a rich deep golden color of the native wood.

As Michael stood there awed and speechless, he turned his light to his left next to John. He saw scratched in cracked letters, "may be at least God will see". Michael thought to himself, how thoughtless he had been to ignore John and his work. John was buried in a pauper's grave on the East End of town. Yet to this day, the Esperson Building remains as an example of high Victorian architecture. It has been declared a historical landmark in large part due to the woodwork of John, a simple man from Portsmouth.

PILGRIM JOURNEY

In the early 1700's, England was a land filled with great strife. Religious factions fought bitterly for control of the land. Many wars and countless years of diabolical political intrigue plagued the land. Civil war is particularly insidious, as it split families and pitted father against son, brother against brother. Great sadness stalked the land, as many a mother's son shed his blood for each side. All of this was done in the name of God, king and country. Many people became embroiled in the fury of the day and many were to give their life to appease the bloodletting. Yet, even more would choose to flee the chaos for a promise of a better life in the New World, even though there were great dangers inherent in the perilous sea voyage across angry seas.

Such was the nature of these times. On a cold dismal October day, the good ship H.M.S. New Hope lay quietly in her berth in Dover Harbor. Her cargo was textiles and manufactured goods bound for Providence in the Colonies. Her Captain was Barnibus Mac Gill, a crusty seaman of 52 years. He had made this passage many times before and knew the route well. He also knew well the fury of the winter gales of the North Atlantic. He respected them, having nearly run aground on his last trip to the Colonies. He also knew, that he must depart soon or be caught in the peak gale season upon his arrival in the colonies. He was concerned. The main deck of his ship would be little more than fifteen feet above the waves even in the calmest of seas. A large swell, if it caught her at the wrong angle in full sail, could easily capsize or de-mast her. These storms were not to be trifled with. His concern was very real!

The H.M.S. New Hope was his ship and was all he owned. He knew her well and enjoyed each sound she made as she rolled in the waves. He had been with her on the maiden voyage and it was he who had majority ownership in her. All these years, he had great comfort in her, she was all he knew and she was his home and his friend. They had fought off pirates, as well as outran the French raiders together many times. He held great pride knowing that he had outrun them. She was a good ship. To him it seemed as though she was impregnable. In his eyes, she was the stateliest gracious lady he knew, and he loved her. Having never married, she was his friend, his mistress and his wife. And beautiful she was indeed. Painted royal blue trimmed in yellow and built of the finest British brown oak. Her forecastle was painted a slightly darker color of blue and was set off with gold highlighted carved details. Her sails were crisp and clean. Her flag fluttered brilliantly in the wind. She struck a fine silhouette against the dingy gray backdrop of the harbor. Her golden figurehead seemed to glisten in the morning sun that day when they were to set sail for the New World. He loved every inch of her. Her rich white sails excited him when he was at the helm under sail. It seemed as though no other thing existed in the world except him, his ship and the sea.

Three days before they were to set sail for Providence; it was decided to take on a few passengers, to defray the cost of the trip. This was a commercial venture and the ship's ledgers would welcome any additional revenue. Lady Wentworth was the first passenger. She was a stately lady of singularly inextricable beauty. Her hair was long and golden yellow. Her eyes were a deep rich blue. She came from one of the finest families of England, her father having been a baron of quite some standing. Yet her life had become hard. For a woman of 23 she had lived through many tragedies. Not long after her father's death, her husband was killed in a duel protecting her honor. The once rich estate had quickly fallen into disrepair and eventually into the hands of unscrupulous men who cheated her of her inheritance. Then to cover their crimes, they spread slanderous rumors at the court, which had caused her to fall from favor with the Queen. The Queen, in her vanity, banished her from the realm to the Colonies in North America.

The day when the New Hope set sail, Lady Wentworth was filled with great fear and trouble. She had never known want and had always lived a well-serviced life. She remembered the rich banquets she once reigned over in Wentworth Manor. How she longed for the pomp and ceremony of the court, yet all she could see ahead of her was danger in a savage new land. That day when she boarded the ship, she knew that she would never return to her beloved England. She brought with her only her clothing and her jewels, both of which she cherished more than life itself. They were all that she had to remind her of her past life that she so longed for. It was all that comforted her as she fled in disgrace to make a new life in the Americas. She could not forget the past and she made resolve that she would not remain poor in the colonies. She took all that she owned and her loyal maidservant Susan with her as she left for the ship that day.

Henry Cox was the second person to book passage on the New Hope. When he boarded, he brought with him a few well-worn clothes and a trunk that held all the tools of his trade. Henry had been a craftsman in Coventry. He had labored many years through internship to become a master carpenter. He had wanted to open his own shop and to prosper in Coventry, his home, but fate would deal him a cruel blow from which he could not recover. He married Jenny Brady at an early age and they were blessed with a child. Not soon thereafter, Henry opened the shop and was prospering, when Jenny fell ill. She contracted tuberculosis and after a costly and lengthy illness, died. Henry's grief was almost unbearable. He took his son to live with his brother, whose wife was childless, and began to drink heavily. In a short time, he found himself hopelessly in debt and facing debtor's prison. He was faced with a cruel choice that he did not want to make. He knew well that all that waited for him in debtor's prison was death. So he reluctantly signed a contract to become an indentured servant and to seek a new life in the Americas. He departed this day with mixed feeling and great loneliness for is lost wife. This was a sad passage, but he had hope that perhaps something greater awaited him in the New World.

The third person to board the ship that day was Robert Mc Phearson. Robert had been in trouble all his life. He had grown up in the ghetto of Glasgow. Orphaned at an early age. It seemed as though a dark cloud followed him wherever he went. He was being pursued by His Majesties' police for stealing and had managed to make his way to Dover without being caught. Robert wanted so much to find a new life. He had no home and thought only to escape. He sold everything he owned and picked a few pockets along his way to acquire passage for the voyage. He boarded that day carrying only a small bundle of clothing and his father's watch, the only thing he had of value. He had sold it many times and then retrieved it with a quick hand before he could be caught. He had longed for the day when he might find riches and become someone of importance. At last, he thought his chance had come. The New World offered inexorable opportunity. The word on the street was that the streets were paved with gold, and all you had to do to get some was to pluck it out of the streams. He was excited about the prospects of getting wealthy, but also apprehensive about the long dangerous sea journey. He could swim well and the thought of all that water, the sea serpents and the storms weighed heavily on his mind, but not so heavily as the thought of being hung by His Majesties Police should he be caught. He boarded that day with some relief and great apprehension.

The last passenger was Master George Whitney. George was a mercantile merchant in London, who had lived many rich years. His business prospered and he was able to enjoy a comfortable life. He had been a very hard workingman. It seemed as though he never quite found time for a family, after all of his business interest required much effort and time. Now that he was advanced in age, he decided to spend his last years in travel. Having already seen Paris, Vienna, Munich and Zurich he sought one last grand adventure in seeing the New World. He also knew, he probably would not return from this trip, since it took three difficult months to make the trip across the great northern ocean and he was already well advanced in age. When the day came to embark, he found himself troubled. He had this urge to find adventure, yet he longed for the comforts of his warm house in Chelsea. When the day of departure came, he simply could not leave his business interests and his home. On the day of the departure, he sent a messenger to Captain Barnibus canceling his passage. The captain was furious. He had already delayed over three hours, nearly missing the tide. He refused to refund passage and made haste to cast off.

The fog burned off quickly that morning when Capt. Barnibus gave the order to hoist the main sail and catch the tide. The crew was all in a flutter around our travelers, whom seemed to only be in the way. It was important to catch the morning tide and the wait for Sir Whitney had delayed him. Each of the passengers stood silently on the fore deck staring back wistfully at the slip as they pulled away. As the New Hope made way for the open sea, each one of them silently wept (in their own fashion) for their circumstances and feared for the uncertainty of their ultimate destination.

The first few weeks of the passage were uneventful. The westerly was strong and the New Hope made good time. But Captain Barnibus knew that this was only foreshadowed by the calm before the winter storms. Shortly thereafter, the cool sunny days faded into cold gray anonymity. The spray of the ocean froze to the decks and the trip became crueler by the day. Our passengers, after a time, became accustomed to the cold. Yet the pitching of the ship seemed to allude their land-bound feet. They were to loose more than one meal to the lack of sea legs.

When the first storm hit the ship, everyone braced for it and although they had expected it, the storm was not welcomed. It hit with such a fury that it shredded the main sail and tore away the crow's nest. Two men were lost in the next few days trying to repair the damage in the driving storm. As the days wore on it became evident that they must turn south or be torn apart by the storm's fury. The Captain knew that this would cost them another month, but he also knew that the only other choice was to break up at sea. So, they reluctantly turned south in hopes of an easier passage clear of the storms in a calm sea. The further south they sailed, the better the weather became. Fortune was with them and the storms subsided. December was normally the most difficult season for the weather and the Captain knew that as soon as they turned north again they would once again encounter the anger of the northern winds. This was not a prospect that he looked forward to. Unfortunately, there would be no other choice, as their present track would bring them into the Carolinas, much too far south. He had to plan a careful course to avoid the Channel Islands and the sand bars that had delayed his last trip by several weeks when he nearly ran aground. He made resolve to stay at least one day off the coast on the northern leg of the trip up to New England. This would avoid the sand bars but might well put them into the eye of another storm. With luck, this might not happen. He knew that if he managed to avoid storms the first week and a half up the coast, he should be clear, as the storms tended to become weaker and less frequent the closer he got to the Hudson River Basin.

They turned north in mid-January. They traveled along the coast of the Carolinas and Virginia, hoping that the land would break the fury of the storms. Again, good luck was with them as they had only the slightest difficulty in making headway. As they neared New York Harbor, they were unexpectedly caught in a large storm from the west. It was the hardest storm they had yet experienced. Uncontrollably they were driven eastwards back into the Atlantic and then northwards towards Nantucket. In the twelfth day of the storm, the main mast was broken four feet below the topsail. It came down with such force, it broke away a good portion of the fore deck destroying the compass and badly damaging the wheel. Captain Barnibus knew that they were in great danger.

They were too near land to drop anchor and ride out the storm. If they remained here they would be torn apart. Then rudder was torn away later that afternoon. This meant that they would have to steer the ship with block and tackle from below deck. This was very difficult work, but it would allow steerage, though admittedly with very slow response. Later in the day, the forecastle was almost stripped clean of rail by the force of the waves, by the wash over of a barnacle-encrusted log. It was swept over and carried two men to their deaths. By now more than half of the ships' sail was ripped beyond repair. In all his years he had never, known of a storm which struck with such fury with waves so high. The size of the demon possessed waves demanded ever more from his ship as the storm went into its 15th day. When the main hatch gave way, the ship began to take on water and the Captain knew that he must take immediate action. He was not exactly sure where they were (not having seen the stars in some weeks and with the compass smashed), yet he knew that he must turn land ward or perish. With a half rudder rigged, they turned land ward on the 16th day of the storm.

Within a half a day, land was sighted and furious preparations were made for landing. When the old lighthouse off Nantucket was sighted, a sigh of relief spread through the crew and passengers. Then about dusk, it seemed as though the storm had subsided slightly. It was decided to try to make harbor. Just as they approached the mouth of the harbor, a furious squall came upon them from the south blowing them toward the jetty. Only the masterful steering of Captain Barnibus saved them from tearing out the bottom of the ship on its jagged stones. Yet, still a new peril waited them on the beach.

As the squall intensified, the remaining portion of the main sail mast was shattered and came crashing down through the first two decks. The wind tossed the ship like a paper boat in a bottle, until the jerry-rigged rudder finally was torn away again. Captain Barnibus knew that there was nothing left that he could do to save his ship, and he went into his cabin to gather up his charts and records, while the crew made way with the lifeboats. The wind quickly smashed several of them against her side splitting them into kindling. The crew began to jump overboard directly into the water. As the wind drove the New Hope onto the rocks, she gave out a groan as though she were dying, The Captain felt as though a wood shard had been thrust into his heart. He felt as though he were dying with her (she was all he had and he still loved her so.)

It was only moments after she hit the rocks; Captain Barnibus gave the order to abandon ship. With no lifeboats left, it was everyone for themselves. Lady Wentworth was frantic as she ran to her cabin to claim her jewelry. She grabbed one of her small chests and her finest cloak. She then ran to the poop deck. There she looked on hopelessly at Captain Barnibus and asked for help. He screamed gruffly, "Jump, woman, jump, for there are no boats left." She hesitated as the ship lurched sharply to the starboard, and then back monetarily righting itself. This threw her off balance and she tumbled to the deck. Still clinging to her chest and robe, she was swept into the raging sea. Her screams could not be heard over the howl of the wind. She was so weighed down by her rich velvet cloak and her jewels; she was quickly pulled to her death.

Robert took the confusion of the moment to find the wealth for which he so long had waited. He rushed to Lady Wentworth's cabin and filled his pockets with the remaining jewels. He grabbed large handfuls of diamond and emerald jewelry and thrust them into his shirt. As the ship lurched sharply to port, he wheeled around and made his way back to the deck. The ocean's fury was so immense; he found it difficult to walk against the wind to the port side rail. As he made his way over the side and into the surf, he was confident that he had finally made it in life. He swam well, but the riptide was too much for him. He fought with all his might to swim to shore, but was pulled helplessly out to sea. Unable to break the tide's pull for the weight of the jewels in his pockets he was dashed against the rocks of the jetty and drowned there. His body was to wash up on the beach some days later, stripped of every jewel by the angry surf.

At the same time as Robert made his way to Lady Wentworth's cabin, Harvey Cox was kneeling in prayer on the remaining portion of the foredeck. He removed his coat, his shirt, and his shoes and threw them into the sea. He threw his tools into the water, which quickly consumed them. Just as he jumped from the rail into the ocean, the New Hope broke in half spewing out all its cargo into the ocean. Henry grabbed a muslin wrapped floating crate and clung to it. He clamored on top of the crate and hung on for his life. He road the waves over the stones as the crate bore the blunt of their force. Each stroke of his arms pulled him closer to safety, as the wind roared its anger against him. Exhausted and almost breathless, he landed on the beach.

After a short time, he stood up and looked back at the New Hope, now only a shattered hulk being consumed by the angry water. Captain Barnibus could be seen standing on the fore deck screaming madly as he was swallowed by the sea. The Captain went down with the ship he so dearly loved. Henry fell to his knees in exhaustion on the beach. The wind drove the waves over him as though they were trying to drag him back into the angry sea. As he crawled toward the inner dunes, he could not help but think how foolish the other passengers had been. The roar of the gale wind was so furious it blotted out all else as he collapsed at the foot of the second dune. He thought to himself how fortunate it was that he had made it to shore. He remembered the many times his father had told him to remember what was of greatest value, much like the proverbs of old. He just lay there regaining his breath.

All hands were lost that day except for Henry Cox who had forsaken every thing he owned to save his life. The people of Nantucket found him curled up shivering by the dune. The lighthouse keeper welcomed him into his home where he was nursed back to health. When his strength returned, he was given new clothes and 20 shillings by the townspeople. He went into Nantucket where he made a new life for himself. He had survived the wreck of the New Hope to become a prosperous carpenter in the New World. He lived to a ripe old age and to this day, his family name is carried on by many grandchildren.

CHAPTER 3

Spinning the Cocoon

There comes a time when we must withdraw from the ever changing, ever turning, ever moving world around us to spin a cocoon, that is ever turning, ever spinning, ever working, like a circle within it's own, building, rolling upon itself, we build a shelter from the storms we know will come.

BOB CAT

Alleksandr Gotslieb moved from his native Poland to Manila in the Philippines in 1938 to take a teaching position at the San Carlos finishing school. Alex had become a well-known mathematician among the educational circles of Europe. He was working hard on what one-day would become to be called fractal geometry, the basis of chaos theory. But, that was yet many years away. The cold weather had taken a large toll on his bones. He could no longer withstand the weather and the flare up in his arthritis that it brought. In addition, there was great trouble brewing in Europe. War clouds were gathering over Europe, and Alex was not excited about remaining near the heat of battle.

When Madam Maria Contadina, the head mistress of the school met him in Vienna at an Educational Conference, she was instantly impressed with his bearing, demeanor and his intellectual stature. But she could not pronounce his name so she called him Alex. He was very well qualified, holding a PHD in Theoretical Mathematics from the University of Vienna. Also he was a fine figure of a man, he stood 6'-2" tall, had short blond hair, blue eyes, and a neatly trimmed sandy colored mustache. Maria decided she absolutely must have him for her school if she was to continue to attract the wealthy European patriarch's children who lived in the Manila area. She had difficulty convincing him to leave the pleasures of Europe for the remote jungle land (or so he thought). She assured him Manila was indeed civilized, as well as a cultured community of which he would become a venerated part as a member of her prestigious school.

Alex's trip to Asia was uneventful. Although seasickness and an occasional storm kept it from being pleasurable, at least it was tolerable. Traveling first class at the expense of the school did have its advantages. Alex loved the amenities that this life style brought to him, though he fully expected to loose them when he arrived at the school. When he arrived in Manila Bay in January 10th of 1938, he was more than ready to disembark. Madam Contadina met him at the dock and escorted him to the school in the school carriage.

When they arrived at the school, Alex was delighted to be met by a cadre of bronze skinned servants who escorted him to his quarters to freshen up. They waited hand on foot on him, much to his delight. After a quick shower and a refreshing glass of cold lemonade, he was shown about the campus. Everything he saw delighted him. The openness of the buildings, (which allowed for ample ventilation) were a pleasing contrast to the cold gray sterility of his native Warsaw winters. He particularly loved the full richness of the tropical garden. There were hundreds of varieties of flowers blooming in profusion all over the grounds. The warm sultry air was scented with the delicate smells and sounds of the tropics. He was a nearly carried away by the sweet smell of the abundant flowers. He thought to himself, this is going to be a wonderful place to live, and so warm I should never have trouble with my arthritis again!

Alex's first year at the Academy was a delight filled experience. He soon found out all the fears of a dangerous and savage environment faded away in the opulence of Manila's high society. Alex very much so liked playing the part of the intellectual. There were dozens of beautiful eligible bachelorettes buzzing around him at all of the schools social functions. He dearly loved all the attention. He thought to himself, he had finally died and gone to heaven. Life was good and there was nothing that he wanted for.

Early in June of his second year at the Academy, he met and fell blindly in love with Rosemary Espinosa. She was the daughter of a wealthy rubber baron. She was every bit an aristocrat. She had waist length silky brown hair. Her eyes were as deep as the night sky. Alex trembled when he touched her golden skin. Her breasts were full and large. She was delicate and very shapely. Every bit of her filled him with delight. She was elegant and well educated. She spoke softly and with great culture. She loved to travel and spoke often of her many trips to Australia, China and Europe. After a short courtship, they were married the following August.

They disembarked at the end of the month for a world honeymoon cruise. Madame Contadina was reluctant to allow Alex to leave the school, even for a short time. She feared that if he ever left he would not return. He was the most valuable teacher that she had, and she knew that if he left fully a third of the students might not return to the school the next session if he were not there. Yet, she also knew well that a love blind man was also of no use to her. Reluctantly, she granted his request for a 3-month sabbatical with his assurances (and a signed contract) that he would return to teach at the school in time for the fall semester.

Alex and Rosemary's trip around the world was a delightful voyage. They really didn't see much of the world, because they were so much in love with each other that they hardly even noticed the world around them. That is, except that horrible day when they watched as a German U-boat shelled and sink an unarmed British Merchantman off the coast of Madagascar. My God, it was horrible and they could do nothing as neutrals. War clouds had gathered over Europe and Asia and were exploding around them. Until then, all of the saber rattling seemed so remote. It was not difficult to predict that a major war was about to engulf the entire world. But, the lovers were consumed with each other at the moment as was not any of their concern.

Europe was abruptly dropped from the tour when The German Army marched into Poland. Alex very much wanted to show his new love the ancestral home. That was now impossible, as it would have to wait for a better time. Needless to say, it was dangerous to travel. Despite the fact that the vessel was flying a neutral flag, the risk was too great to travel the north. The ships company wisely decided to remain in the Southern Hemisphere, thinking it much safer being far from the winds of war.

Alex was deeply disturbed to hear of the fall of his beloved Warsaw and greatly worried for his family there. He, along with all of the rest of the world was shocked by the blitzkrieg speed with which Poland was crushed. But, now he was as much Phillippino as Polish. He felt, as did Rosemary, that the war would never touch them, after all Manila belonged to the United States of America, the strongest nation in the world. No one would dare attack them! Besides it was 10,000 miles form Europe, who would bother. To further place their minds as rest, Japan was preoccupied with China. No one would dare attack, it was just unthinkable.

It was early September 1941 when they sailed slowly back into placid Manila Bay. The silhouette of the Old Spanish fort was a comforting sight for homesick Rosemary and Alex. As they arrived at the Academy, Madame Contadina presented Alex with a small yellow cat wrapped in an oversized yellow bow. This was a home coming gift, which was very well received. The head mistress hoped it would also encourage them to settle on the grounds of the school, rather than find a home downtown. Alex was a cat lover and this blue-eyed yellow fur ball absolutely delighted him. After a modest resistance, Rosemary reluctantly agreed to let it became a part of the family. Alex named the cat an unceremonious Bob.

In no time at all they were back into the hub of the Manila's social life. Alex was busily teaching at the school and Rosemary delighted herself making a home for them. They selected a modest white bungalow not far from the school near the main railroad station. Early the next month, Rosemary announced to Alex that she was pregnant. Alex could scarcely contain his excitement. In his delight, he bought a case of fine Havana cigars and passed them out to everyone he met, despite the fact that it was a full seven months before the child would be born. Rosemary managed to keep her composure despite all the excitement. Really, though she enjoyed all the flurry of attention as Alex tried to meet her every whim (in the hopes of making things easier for her). She would be due the following spring. Alex could not wait but Rosemary was apprehensive. Having a first child had been difficult for her mother and also her grandmother. She was concerned that perhaps she too might lose the baby. But, she did not tell this to Alex, as she did not want to dampen his happiness.

When December 6 came and Alex made his way to the school. As he passed the train station, he noticed a large black pall of smoke coming from the horizon, near the U.S. Naval Base. Not thinking, he mused to himself that some hotshot pilot must have really blown it. He made an off-handed silent bet with himself that the pilot had hit the naval oil reserves instead of the targets in the sea beyond. Boy was that guy in deep trouble, he thought. December 6 was going to be a busy Saturday, he thought to himself. First its the coming out party for Doronda Nurvise, at the school, at 9 am, then at noon the luncheon for the Hibiscus club scholarship fund and at 3 p.m. it was back to school for Martha Glories 15th year celebration and coming out party. This was a day to remember for all these young girls. There was so much to do to prepare and not enough time to get it done. He rushed as he moved down the street.

Just as Alex started across the main square, an airplane zoomed low over him at tree top level. Looking up he saw a white single engine craft that seemed to him to be a fighter. Looking down again at his newspaper, he continued to walk across the square. Then ka-plow! An explosion sent him reeling back toward the curb showering him with bits of broken cobblestones and dirt. He was dazed for a moment and sat stunned on the pavement. Then a second plane dove in on the square, this time with its machine guns blazing. People ran panicked for cover, as it flew down the main street raising two parallel lines of death. Alex ducked for cover. A cab ran abruptly up onto the sidewalk lurching to a stop and exploding in a ball of flames against the train station. "My God" Alex screamed out loud, "they are attacking us!" No sooner than he had said that, than another explosion set the church at the north end of the square on fire, knocking its spire into a heap of rubble in the street. Alex jumped to his feet ran back toward his house. By now bombs were falling all around him. Everywhere there were screaming children and running people. Several people lay motionless bleeding in the street. It was absolute chaos. People were running everywhere and nowhere. There were dozens of injured and dying people lying in the streets, as fire engines and ambulances darted back and forth.

By the time he got past the train station, panic had broken out there also. Dozens of planes were flying back and fourth over the marshaling yards strafing and bombing the tracks. The 9:15 just in from the upper island run, was derailed and burning at the east end of the station platform. People were running in every direction unable to find safety anywhere. Thick black smoke obscured his view as an ambulance careened down the street toward the station. Alex made his way through the cratered street hoping to find his home safe. As he rounded the corner, he could see his house completely engulfed in flames. Fernando the gardener was standing near the front door hopelessly trying to fight the fire with a tepid garden hose. When Alex ran breathlessly to his side, he turned weeping and said "Rosemary, Rosemary, My God she's still in there".

Alex was frantic. He tried four times to enter the house, but the smoke and fire was too intense, driving him back desperately gasping for air. Finally, Fernando had to knock him out with the handle of a rake to keep him from perishing in the flames himself. He woke up later that evening on the floor of Madam Contadina's living room with Bobcat purring gently on his stomach. All around him were the sounds of weeping children and people crying out in pain. Madaia had converted her schoolhouse into an impromptu hospital. Alex soon lost himself in the rush to save lives as the flow of casualties rapidly increased. There wasn't much that he could do, he was not a medical doctor, but he used whatever first aid he could remember to do what he could as the hours droned into days.

As the battle for the city raged into its third day, Alex hardly noticed the roar of the fighting was getting closer and closer. Despite some shells landing uncomfortably close in the courtyard, breaking the windows, he continued working. This was how it was until the morning of the fourth day, when machine gun fire broke down the front door killing one of the attendants. Lieutenant Atsumi entered the house preceded by seven soldiers and announced that everyone was a prisoner of the Japanese Imperial Army. No one objected for fear of being shot. Lieutenant Junji Atsumi walked up to Alex, who was almost twice his size, and thrust a bayonet up into his face and said, "You, Yankee, you are to come with me."

Alex was dragged bodily out into the courtyard, where fourteen other Anglos were being guarded by half a dozen soldiers at bayonet point. Alex was so tired from the many days of sleepless hospital work and the shock of his wife's death, he offered no resistance. The almost consistent 24-hour a day of hospital duty had left him so exhausted that it was everything he could do to just to stand up. After waiting for almost three and a half hours, standing in the hot courtyard, all of the Anglos were marched at a quick step to the precinct jail now converted to a military detention center. They were forced into an already over crowded cell and left there. As the door closed behind them with a loud clank, Alex could not help but think that he would never see the sunlight again. Three weeks later a military guard came to the cell and called out Alex's name. His heart dropped, he thought for sure that he was going to be summarily shot, as executions were being performed regularly. He was escorted at bayonet point to the office of the Commander of that sector, Major Katana Tanaga.

Alex was informed through an interpreter, he had already been tried and found guilty by a military tribunal of crimes against the people. The newly liberated nation of Philippines required him to pay the penalty of twelve years at hard labor for exploiting the people. When Alex objected, saying he was a civilian and that Major Tanaga had no authority to try him in this manner, he was interrupted by a swift butt stroke from his guard's rifle to his ribs. The stroke took his breath away and cracked two ribs. Major Tanaga retorted quickly in broken Filipino, "You have only the rights that I give to you, Yankee dog." Alex protested he was Polish, but his words fell on deaf ears.

Early the next morning he was escorted to military prison number eight, along with 195 other civilian prisoners. Prison Camp number eight was located in an isolated jungle area just west of Manila. It wasn't much more than a barbed wire compound in which men were held. There were three wire fences each encircling the other. Each one was taller than the one preceding it. The outer perimeter was marked with twine and white markers. The prisoners were told these markers designated a minefield and escape was impossible. They were given a few poles and some palm branches and were told to build themselves shelter. Military prisoners were separated from the civilians and the officers were completely isolated from the rest of the group in a separate section of the compound. Lt. Col. Kamatzu was the commander of the camp. He was a ruthless man who swore that no man would survive if he attempted to escape his camp.

In the next 24 months nearly seventy-five men perished in trying to gain their freedom or from starvation and disease. In addition to the escapees being beheaded, Lt. Col. Kamatzu had the prisoners that slept to the left and the right of the escapees shot as well. Morale was very low among the prisoners. All hope of survival seemed to vanish as Alex went into the twenty-fifth month of his captivity. He lost nearly 87 pounds and was almost too weak to perform the work tasks that were assigned to his group on the road gang. The penalty for failing in that day's quota was the firing squad.

The gruel that they were fed once a day consisted of very few bits of rice and abundant straw. By the end of the month, almost two thirds of the prisoners were too weak to stand. Dysentery and malaria alone were killing an average of twelve men a week. There seemed to be a constant stream of prisoners coming to the camp and no new facilities were being built. There were no doctors and the prisons were so over crowded, they literally slept on top of each other.

When August began, Alex was on the verge of cracking. Lack of food, incessant heat, mosquitoes, and constant harassment by the guards had taken the spirit out of him. Alex had never been a religious man, but he did remember the church lessons he learned in catholic preparatory school when he was a child in Warsaw. He had reached his end. Alex did not know what else to do. So, late the night of August 4th, he fell to his knees and cried out to God in his desperation. "God, if you are up there," he said through his tears, "help me, help me!" He collapsed on the floor in his tears exhausted and fell asleep waiting for death.

Early the next morning just as the sun had begun to bring the jungle alive, it occurred to Alex that he was still alive. A wet nose against his cheek awakened Alex. He lurched back thinking that it was a rat looking for breakfast, but much to his surprise it was Bob, his cat. Bob jumped back a few steps, then walked slowly up to Alex purring rubbing himself on Alex's leg. Bob curled himself around Alex's weak legs, stroking back and forth like he wanted something to eat. Alex smirked to himself; if he had anything to eat he sure would not give it to a cat!

But, Alex was so pleased to see his lost friend, he didn't even think of how Bob got there. They sat there rejoicing in a small bit of pleasure in the darkness. He finally smiled for the first time in this bleak environment. As Alex would scratch Bob's ear, Bob in turn would nibble on Alex's fingers and purr loudly. After a few minutes, Bob began to fidget which mystified Alex, as Bob was usually a very sedentary animal. Alex picked up Bob and placed him in his lap. Bob jumped immediately out of Alex's lap and scurried quickly out the door. When Alex didn't follow, Bob returned to the door, peered around the corner and began to meow loudly. Alex was delighted to see Bob again, but was concerned that someone else would hear him and Bob might end up in the evening soup. Alex got up as quick as his weakened condition would allow. When he did, Bob pranced off toward the north edge of the camp fence with his tail straight up in the air. Every two or three steps, Bob would turn around to make sure that Alex was still following.

When they reached the fence, Bob stopped and circled something lying still in the grass. It was a dead green parakeet. Alex looked at the bird and began to weep. In the following months, Bob continued to bring small rodents, dead lizards and birds to Alex every morning. Alex was there to greet Bob with a gentle scratch between the ears. All Bob seemed to want was a scratch then he would scurry back into the jungle again. This continued almost every day for months. When the American army liberated Manila some time later, Alex was one of the few prisoners who survived from the beginning of the war in a concentration camp.

Alex and Bob returned to the San Carlos school. Over the next few years they were inseparable as they strove to rebuild it. To this day, he teaches there as head master. Although Bob has long since passed into the hands of the Master, Alex still remembers the day he cried out to the God for help. He remembers well how faithfully that a small cat, named Bob, brought him birds and rodents to eat. It was these meager offerings that provided the necessary protein that he needed to survive. He marveled how it took a small yellow cat to show him how big God really was.

A QUIET YOUNG MAN

R ob Miller was a quiet young man. He rarely raised his voice and almost never lost his temper. That was a good thing, because by the time he got into high school he was a 6'-4", 215 pound stack of muscle. He enjoyed bodybuilding and spent a lot of time at the gym during those high school years. He was never known to have a mean streak and was often credited (and justly so) for going out of his way to defend the weak in the many small skirmishes that go on during the breaks between classes at high school

In his early years, Rob grew up in the farming community of Planda, California. He moved with his family at the age of six to the farm his father bought near Tulare, California. His father, Fredrick was a strong tall hard working quite man of Swedish descent. He never said much, you just kind of knew what he had in mind. I suppose this is where Rob got his silent streak. Rob's dad came from the old school where you worked from sun up to sunset to coax the crops from the fields and you never complained. That was the way he was raised. Fredrick, Rob and his two younger brothers worked a relatively small 150-acre farm in the central San Joaquin Valley. They had nearly 70 acres of almond trees, 50 acres of wall nuts and ran 25 dairy cattle on the remaining 30 acres. Rob's mother always demanded a 5 acre or so garden and some fruit trees. There were always plenty of fresh vegetables, canned goods and homemade jellies around the house. Everyone worked very hard on the land to coax it to bear its goodness, but no one seemed to mind.

Running cattle on the small remaining acreage was always hard. Fredrick managed to lease another 100 acres from the adjacent farm for grazing. But, there was never enough natural silage for the cattle. That meant Rob, his dad and his brothers were constantly going somewhere to buy, buck and store hay. Not much was ever said on these many trips up and down the valley. It was just not Fredrick's way. The boys understood and most often by the time they were 15 minutes down the road, all three were either fast asleep or reading a book. There was always a lot of hard physical work associated with these trips, so Fredrick did not mind them getting a little extra rest when they could.

In the late fall of 1968, Rob got a draft notice to report to the Army recruiter for a physical. Rob went without hesitation or reservation. He had been reared on a strong diet of love in the home, love for the land and patriotism. He genuinely loved America and despite a raft of anti-war media attention, he willingly went to Vietnam to protect democracy. A lot of his classmates thought this was corny, but Rob did not care, and quite frankly no one dared say anything to him about it anyway, at least not in front of him.

Rob's 14 months of basic and specialty training went faster than most of the troops wished it would. Rob, being true to his nature, volunteered to be a battlefield medic. It was very dangerous duty. He knew it and volunteered just the same. He felt it was the right thing to do. During his first tour of duty he was credited with saving the lives of dozens of his fellow battalion members. Rob never bragged about it and never told anything to his mom and dad about what he was doing. He knew his mother would only worry and his dad had far too much work to do on the farm with one less set of hands available. Almost imperceptibly at first, then more obviously later, the din of so many firefights began to take a toll on Rob. He had seen far more violence than any man twice his age should see in ten life times. He got tired of seeing so many mangled bodies and hearing the screaming wounded, but never said anything about it, as it was not his style. He just did his best to save those he could get too.

After his year tour ended, he was ready to come home. He called his parents from Travis Air Force Base Embarkation Point saying, "Mom and Dad, I'm coming home, but I have a real big favor to ask. I have am army buddy from my platoon I'd like to bring with me." Being big hearted for visitors, they replied "Why yes, we'd love to meet any friend of yours." But Rob continued, "there's something you need to know, he was hurt pretty badly in the war. He tripped a Viet Cong booby trap, setting off a land mine. He lost an arm, an eye and most of the fingers on the other hand. He does not have anywhere to go and I want him to come live with us on the farm."

Fredrick was on the extension phone and did not say much, he just scowled. Rob's mother hesitated and then she said, "I'm sorry to hear that son. Maybe we can help him find somewhere to live." Rob responded, "no, Momma, you don't understand, I want him to live with us on the farm." Fredrick finally broke into the conversation when he heard the saddened tone of his wife's voice. He said, "son you don't know what you are asking us to do. I am well past 70 and momma, although she usually says jokingly that she is 18 is not much behind me." Momma, cleared her voice noticeably, at this point, on the other phone. Someone with that kind of handicap would be a terrible burden on us. We have our own lives to live. Your youngest brother just went of to Fresno State and won't be here to help on the farm. We can't handle something like this right now. I think you should just come home and let the Veterans Administration take care of him. They have some really wonderful places for those kinds of folks. It is OK for him to come for a visit, but to stay here permanently is just out of the question. The VA will have a place for him."

At that point the phone connection was interrupted. His parents thought nothing of it, as out in the country interrupted phone conversations were very common. Birds, squirrels and low rural phone maintenance budgets often played havoc with the phone lines. They expected that he would call back shortly, or at least in the next day or so.

When he did not call back after a week, they began to get concerned. So Fredrick made a call the base locator at Travis Air Force Base to see if he could find his son. After some time, they managed to find his battalion commander. Maj. Laverne informed them that Rob had checked out on leave the week before and that he assumed he was going home, but was not quite sure where he went. Rob's mother was frantic, but Fredrick reassured her that he knew Rob was very good hearted and probably was out trying to find some place for his buddy to stay. He assured her that he was confident that Rob would show up in a day or so.

When he did not come home the following week. They were really troubled. It was not uncommon for Rob not to write, he never did that much, and when he did it was never more than a few short lines. That was the way he was, he was quiet and never said much about anything, much less how he felt. They were disturbed that he did not call back. This was the first time that he had failed to call home when he had previously said that he would call. He always called when he was out of town, so as to put mother's mind at rest. This was just not like him.

Late on Monday of the third week, they finally got a call. Fredrick and his wife's hearts raced as they ran to the phone expecting to hear Rob was in route or needed to be picked up from the Greyhound Bus Station in Tulare. But, what they heard was the Fresno Police inform them that their son had died after falling from the seventh floor window of the Tioga Hotel. The police suspected that it was suicide, but they were not exactly sure. The grief-stricken parents flew to Fresno that night and were taken to the city morgue to identify the body the following morning. They recognized him, but to their horror they discovered something they didn't know about their son. He had only one eye, one arm and only two fingers on the other hand. They were both shocked speechless. They took Rob's body home and buried him in the family plot on the farm that he loved so much. Neither of them talked much about it and maybe why it had happened as it did. It was just not their style.

Their grief was immense. Neither could talk about it for many months although both of them were racked by pain. Finally on the first anniversary of his death they fell into each other's arms and truly cried. They decided right then and their that they would not let another mother or another father suffer as they had. The decided to sell the farm, retire and using the proceeds form the sale to open a half way house for paraplegics. Fredrick never said much about it after the decision was made. He just did it. And his wife became mother to dozens of hurt but healing young people who had nowhere else to turn.

THE GREAT SNOW OF 1889

The weather in the year 1889 was extremely unusual. It seemed for some odd reason the seasons got all mixed up. The eastern seaboard had a particularly mild spring and a very dry summer. The center of the nation was just the opposite, although this type of weather was not uncommon. What was surprising was that it lasted for several months, rather than several days. Everyone in Windrock, Nebraska were used to the wild changes in the weather caused by Chinook winds coming off the Rockies. What they were not used to, however, was the strange and sometimes violent shifts that lasted for weeks and even months.

As one might guess, this type of weather was particularly hard on the farmers. The spring wheat had all but been wiped out by the torrents of early rain. Every creek had overflowed their banks and most of the river bottom pastures were too soggy for the cattle to graze. The soil just plain had too much water in it. The plantings roots rotted before they could gain enough strength to get more than a few inches above the ground. It seemed whenever it was about to dry out; another freak thunderstorm would dump an inch or two of fresh rain. The crops were ruined. If it were not for the truck gardens every farmer planted near their house, and the canning done the year before, most of them would have been in dire straits.

Mini Freeman was an English immigrant who had come to the Great Plains some five years earlier. Minerad Cyble Freeman the Third was her given name, but most people found it much too difficult to pronounce so they called her Mini. She attended the Normal School in Enid, Oklahoma to obtain her teaching certification. After several interviews, she finally settled on a teaching position in Windrock. Well it was not exactly in Windrock. She was responsible for teaching the farm children north of Windrock. Her one room schoolhouse was located at Pierce Creek some twenty-five miles north of Windrock and one hundred seventy-five miles away from anything else. It was built on top of a hill using gyp-lap wood planking on a wooden frame. As this was a poor school district, there was no insulation only coal oil lamps and a two-hole privy out back. The schoolhouse was little more than a wooden shack with a pot-bellied stove, a black board and wooden benches. She was responsible for teaching grades two through nine. After that, the children were expected to go to the school in the city or they could simply remain on the farm to help their parents with the crops.

As was the custom of the day, classes did not begin until all of the crops were in. That could be anywhere from mid August to late November depending on the size of the crops and well, the weather. This year, as you might expect, classes started early. It was not much of a class, as there were only six students registered. Fortunately, there had apparently been a particularly cold winter in times past, as all but one of the children were about the same age. All but Jenny Langtree were in the seventh grade. Jenny was the youngest and was in the third grade. There was also Brian Wilson, who was particularly large for is age being nearly six-foot tall and a bit slow. He had apparently been held back a couple of grades, as he did not seem to get his ciphering right.

Mini enjoyed the solitude of the school. She enjoyed living in the country where she could hear the birds and see the sunshine on the tall buffalo grass. The city was just too dirty, noisy and much too smelly. Mini liked the country, but she was lonely for her ancestral home in Swindon. In an odd sort of way, the area around the school reminded her of South England (although Nebraska was not as green and had far fewer trees.) She missed her family and longed for the low rolling hill where she was born. She had extra time to ponder these things, as all the kids except Jenny were in the same grade. This significantly reduced her teaching chores.

That first day of classes was uneventful. The students, like students everywhere were more interested in what was out the windows than what was on the chalkboard. Mini could not blame them, as it was a cool blustery day and they had been used to being in the fields. It was not easy for them to adjust to being cooped up in a musty drafty old building, which had been boarded up for the last few months. She did her best to teach the rudiments of math, penmanship and reading. Sometimes it was frustrating, as most of the children really did not want to be there. In fact, they excelled only at lunch and recess. That is if you don't count pranks, which they planned meticulously.

On the morning of 20 November, there was nothing particularly different about the day. Mini arrived at 6 am to start the fire in the stove and prepare for the day's lessons. At 7 am the students began to arrive for classes starting at 8 am. Mini noticed that the wind was particularly brisk that day and dark clouds were gathering in the west when she went outside to raise the flag. She thought nothing of it, as the weather had been so difficult these last few months. By the time recess came at 10 am, the wind was whistling through the pickets of the fence that surrounded the schoolyard and the temperature dropped nearly 15 degrees. It was getting colder by the minute. Mini was still not unduly concerned, as the almanac said that winter was expected to be early this year.

When lunch came, the wind was howling through the cracks in the schoolhouse walls. The pot-bellied stove could barely keep up with the cold creeping into the building, despite Mini stoking it regularly. She looked out the window apprehensively, as snow flurries began to fall. How odd, she thought, snowing this early in the year. Within the hour, the flurries had turned to a torrent and the torrent to a full-blown blizzard. By this time, the stove could not keep up with the cold that forced its way into the room. The wind was driving so hard that periodically an errant snowflake would make its way into the room through one of the cracks in the walls. The roof moaned and swayed in the wind. Several times, when there was a particularly hard gust of wind, Mini even thought that she heard some of the roof timbers crack. But, she could not be sure, and hoping for the best, she put that thought out of her mind.

Along about 2 p.m., the wind blew so hard it blew the door open with a loud clatter. A pile of snow flooded into the schoolhouse. The children panicked and rushed to the front of the room. Mini shooed all the children to the center of the building near the still glowing stove. She pushed with all her might against the wind and drift to try to close the door lest they all freeze, but she was not having much luck. Fortunately, Brian saw what was going on and put his shoulder into the door to assist and they managed to close it. This happened twice more before Mini decided to nail the door shut.

The wind continued to build in intensity, until it was all they could hear above the whimpering of the girls surrounding the stove. Buy this time, the blizzard had developed such intensity, it would be impossible for any of the children to make it home alone. Mini decided to hole up in the schoolhouse until the storm ran its course. It was hard to believe that it could happen, but over the next few hours, the weather got even worse. This was particularly uncommon, as blizzards generally wound down when the sunset. By this time, all of the children were securely wrapped in half a dozen layers of clothing, including anything that they could find in the lost and found. Mini was concerned the parents might be worried, but there was no way to contact them, as most lived 10-15 miles or more away and the wind had caused her horse to run off. So, Mini crumpled up the newspapers she was using for reading class and stuffed them in the sleeves and under the coats of the children for extra insulation. They had no choice now but to wait out the storm. But, it got colder still.

The two cords of firewood provided by the school board was quickly consumed. Ice was developing on the inside of the windows and the children were coughing as though they were beginning to get ill. Mini was reluctant to damage school property, but she could see no other way to stay warm. She decided that there was no other choice. She instructed Brian to break up the benches and the desks to burn in the stove (which he did gleefully). The wind howled even louder. It seemed they could barely keep ahead of the freezing wind. As they breathed, their breaths hung suspended in a white cloud in the room unable to dissipate for lack of warmth. By daybreak, most of the furniture had been burned and the blizzard was still howling.

Now, much more worrisome than the door, was the roof that sprang a leak. Snow was filtering into the classroom near the blackboard where the wind had blown the shingles off. Mini could see nothing out the windows. They had frosted over opaque on the inside. The last time the wind blew open the nailed door, she could see it was a complete white out. The blizzard blanketed everything in a surreal blanket of white.

At about 10 am on the second day, or so they thought, we can not be sure, because the gears on her locket watch had frozen, the wind blew the remainder of the roof off the building. The belfry had long ago been torn away and the bell fell into the schoolyard. Mini knew their lives were seriously in danger. She knew she had to act and to act now. She made her way to the cloakroom of the schoolhouse and groped with her bare hands in the snow until she found the end of the bell rope. She pulled with all her might to draw in the rope. It resisted her, as it was tangled in the remains of the belfry. Fortunately, the bell had separated from the rope or she might not have had enough strength to pull it in with the bell attached. She coiled the rope carefully in wide loops in her hand and returned to the pot bellied stove.

She got everyone's attention and said, "Children we are in a serious situation. We need to work together in order to get out of this. The school is no longer safe." Then as to accent her comments a rafter snapped with a loud crack under the weight of the snow on the roof. Snow was now falling into the schoolhouse much faster. As it fell on the stove, it hissed, sending out a large cloud of objecting steam. We have to try to get to widow Plute's house. It is made of stone and has a big fireplace in it. We will be safe there! Brian, you are the biggest so you need to be last in line. I will lead and everyone MUST stay together. If you get lost in the snow there will be no way for us to find you in this blizzard." Mini tied the rope to Brian and then one at a time to each of the children. Last, she tied it to herself and scooped up Jenny into her arms. "Now," she said, "stick together, keep your hands in your pockets and holler if for some reason the rope comes off. Lets say a prayer that we will be safe," which they did. With that she turned and made her way out the door into the snowdrifts with her little train following slowly behind her.

Mini knew that she must find the barbed wire fence that paralleled the road. It wouldn't be easy as the snow completely blinded them. It was the worst white out she had ever experienced. The wind blew incessantly form the northwest. It bit into the uncovered parts of her skin like a thousand knives driving the snow into the flesh. It pounded against their clothing, stealing their body heat. The cold was so heavy, when she breath it seemed to freeze the very air in her lungs before she could exhale. Each breath was painful. Every step was as though she was walking barefoot on broken glass. She was blind, unable to see and barely able to breath. Her lungs ached and her throat seared with each agonizingly cold breath. It was not long before her feet got numb and she could not feel her fingers. The cold was unbelievable.

After what seemed like an hour, but could not have been more than a few moments she heard a large crack and then the sound of splintering wood. The wind and the weight of the snow had finally taken the old school house as it collapsed in to a snow covered pile of rubble. They had just gotten out in time. Sad as it was to loose the school, it did serve an important purpose. Based on the direction of the sound and taking into account the direction and speed of the wind, Mini was able to guess which way to go in order to find the barbed wire fence and the road to widow Plute's house. She considered herself lucky when she tripped over the top strand of wire in the fence now nearly completely covered by the snow.

Picking herself up and brushing off Jenny who was crying, (more from the cold than the surprise of the fall) they proceeded to the east and toward widow Plute's house. It seemed like the wind fought their every step. From time to time, she would look back as the rope went slack for a moment, to see if all the children were still there. That was virtually fruitless, because the wind prevented her seeing more than a few feet before her eyes were filled with snow. So, she tugged on the rope, hoping that someone would tug back. She was thankful for each tug as she continued to fight the wind and the snow.

They were making very slow progress and the wind was getting worse. After an hour of struggling, Mini was exhausted. She decided to stop to take a rest. Just as she was thinking that they should be somewhere near Stillwater Creek, she walked straight into a large tree.

She gasped with relief knowing that indeed she was near the creek; because that is the only place the cotton wood trees grew around those parts. Mini gathered the children on the leeward side of the tree. She reeled in her line like a mother hen counting her chicks. As the rope yielded each child, she reached out and gave them a reassuring hug. She was delighted to see the large shadow of Brian approach her at the end of the rope. Fortunately this tree was wide enough to shield all of them. So they stood there for a while gathering their strength. As soon as she knew then that all of the children were still with her and still safe, and she smiled! She instructed Brian to scoop out an enclosure at the base of the tree under a large root, so that they could get out of the wind. They all arranged themselves carefully in the hole and huddled together for warmth. She thought about lighting a fire, but the wind was too brisk to light a match.

Mini was about spent. She had been cutting the trail against the wind and the snowdrifts, as well as pulling her little reluctant train along. Everyone was tired, bone tired. Everyone was cold, colder than any of them had ever been in their lives. No one could feel their toes and some of them even had blue noses with ice sickles hanging from them. Their breaths had condensed on their scarves and eyebrows in a macabre white crust. Everyone was exhausted and about to give up, except Mini. She rubbed their hands and their arms and slapped them on the backs to get their circulation going again. She tied their scarves tighter and re-wrapped the loosened coats. She did everything she could think of to keep up their spirits and to encourage them. She even promised them a gold star if everyone stuck this one out. She told them all that they were almost at the widow's house. She told them that it was only half a mile down the road (when she knew herself that it was more like three miles). They just had to stick together and they just had to keep going or they would freeze. Starting a fire was out of the question, as no sooner than they dug a small depression to build it in the wind filled it with snow again.

Mini offered another prayer saying, "Alright children, let's pray: Lord help us in our hour of peril send us a guiding angel so we can find a warm place of safety." Shortly thereafter, she rousted her reluctant band and headed down the creek bed, thinking that it might save some time and knowing that the widow's house was within eyeshot of the creek. What she did not know at the time, is that she had become disorientated and was walking away form the house and not toward it. After an hour of struggling through the snow, Mini came to the horrifying conclusion they must have walked past the house, as they should have been there by now. So, without telling the children, she walked them into a wide 180-degree arch and head back down the creek. Because the direction of the wind had shifted, she misjudged the turn and inadvertently headed out over flat pasture. After fifteen minutes of trudging through the snow without seeing a tree, her heart sank. She knew without any landmarks, they were doomed to being lost on the endless expanses of farmland. Mini was about to cry, when a shadow approached her out of the white of the snow.

At first she thought, OH GOD, a wolf because it seemed to leap up out of the snow on all fours. Much to her relief after a moment, she could see the shape of a man materializing from the whiteness as he got up from sitting on a rock. He appeared to be more than seven feet tall and very old. Mini knew that could not be true, but it was hard to get any perspective without anything to compare it to in all that white. The man appeared to be an old gray-headed Indian. He was wrapped in a buffalo blanket and had a bandana around his head with geometric designs in it. He smiled broadly at her, and then taking her by the forearm said, "Follow". He then started to drag her forward to the right. Mini resisted, saying, that cannot be the right way. We should be going this way (tugging to the left.)" The stranger ignored her and pulled her firmly to the right, taking her entire train along with them. After a time, it was all Mini could do just to keep up with the old man and his long steps. All of them trudged through the snow, plowing through one drift after another until they came upon the wire fence again. Mini's heart melted with relief. They had found the road again. Now they were sure to find the house. Ten minutes later, they were at the porch of widow Plute's house.

The old man helped each one of them up on the porch. He used the side of his broad foot to scrape the snowdrift off the porch so the door would open. He then knocked briskly on the door with three loud bangs. Shortly, widow Plute peeked out the window to see who could possibly be out in such horrible weather. She was shocked to see the small crowd on her front porch. It took a couple of minutes to break the ice away from the doorframe so the door could be opened. When they did, all the kids marched in, numbed and cold into the front room where the fireplace was roaring hot. It took only a few moments to shed their now wet dripping, frozen clothing and to gather around the life giving warmth.

Mini was the last into the room and the last to take off her soggy frozen outer garments. Widow Plute put on hot soup and had warm muffins for all of them. Each of the children drank their fill and ate several muffins smothered in fresh butter before Mini noticed that the old man was not with them. She went to the front door to look for him, but she could see but the ever-present blizzard. When she asked widow Plute about the old man, she said that she had not seen anyone but the kids and her. Mini had a chill run down her spine! When she insisted that the old man had been there and he had led them to her house, widow Plute remarked that apparently the cold had dulled your mind! Being lost in blizzards was known to cause you to see strange things, or so widow Plute said. Mini decided to drop the matter unless someone thinks she was crazy and she might lose her job. But she knew in her own heart that her prayer had been answered.

Two and a half days later, the storm broke and the farm people were frantically looking for their children. They discovered the collapsed schoolhouse and feared the worst. When the advance party arrived at widow Plute's house, they all erupted in to joyous thanksgiving for their children's safety. They heaped praise on Mini, who had kept a cool head and used remarkable courage to save them. She was reluctant to take any of the credit, which they marked as her being quite properly modest. To this day, the folks who live around Windrock tell the story of the horrible winter of 1889 and how a small woman saved the children form the killer storm of the century. Mini, for her part, was glad to be of help and is thankful that her prayers were answered.

CHARLES SMITHWORTH
THE THIRD

Late one afternoon, the minister of the largest Protestant church in downtown Minneapolis was walking through the chancery just before lunch and decided that he should pray for inspiration for the Sunday sermon. So he went into the sanctuary to sit down and pray. Just as he did, the side door opened and in walked an aged disheveled man. He hair was scruffy; he was wearing dirty work clothes and clearly needed a shave. His coat was faded and his boots had seen better days. He sat down, bowed his head, staying only a moment, then got up and walked back out the door. How odd, the minister thought as he turned to begin his mediation in preparation for his work.

The same thing happened the following Tuesday, Wednesday and Thursday. He did not come on Friday, but on Saturday and late in the evening he returned. This pattern repeated itself consistently over the next few months. Every lunchtime he was there. He would come in, sit only a moment with his head bowed, then would quickly leave.

The minister could not understand what was going on. He thought perhaps this man was a vagrant and only wanted to warm himself in the church. But, he really did not stay long enough to do that. Perhaps he was lost and trying to find his way home. He came too many times for that to make much sense. Maybe the minister thought, he is a thief and he is trying to case the church for a robbery. Being a good steward of the church property, he decided to confront the man the next day.

When the man came in the following day, he was wearing the same old scruffy clothing, and sat in the same spot. He remained only a few moments with his head bowed. Just as he started to get up to leave, the minister stepped in front of him and asked, "Excuse me mister, what are you doing here!"

The old man introduced himself as Charles Smithworth the Third. By the manner he was speaking, he had apparently been given a very good education, although you could not tell that by the clothing he wore. He was a bit taken back and surprised by the minister whom appeared to sneak up on him. He gathered his composure and explained. I work on the construction crew of the new Pillsbury building as the sweep-up man. Lunch break is only 20 minutes and for me that is prayer time. I use it to find solace and strength. The minister asked him "then why don't you stay longer?" He explained that the work site is a good distance from here and it takes me nearly 9 minutes to walk here and 9 to walk back. I do not make enough money afford to buy a bus pass. So, I pray as I come and as I go. Then when I get here I thank the good Lord for the day. I say, "I came in today to tell you how very happy I have been since I found our friendship and you took away my arrogance. I think about you each and every day and so this is Charles, checking in on you my friend . . . I love you." By the time I do that, it is time to return to work.

The minister was taken aback at the answer, expecting something entirely different. He asked the old man why he did not come to the Sunday services? He answered, "Pastor, look at me. This is such a fine upper class church. These clothes are all that I have I just could not do it. I would be embarrassed to come to such a fine church dressed like this. Besides, I don't think that the parishioners would want me here. I just do not think that I would be welcome.

Charles then said, "I did not always dress like this. I once was a professor at the University of Minnesota. It was a very difficult for my father and our family to climb out of the depression, away from the dust bowl and out of the farm. Our family nearly starved a couple of times. But, my dad always told me to talk to the Lord and he will take care of you. Over the years, I managed to earn my bachelors of Science in Literature and ultimately a Doctorate in Elizabethan

Literature. Because it was so hard to get ahead and it took so much time, I married late in life. Then Marda, God rest her soul, my beloved wife was killed in an automobile accident before we had any children. I sort a fell apart . . . . I miss her so much. She was the heart of my life and my great love." He lowered his head and tried to cover the fact that a tear had come to his eye. "It was not soon there after that I was accused of making improper advances toward one of my students. She filed a totally baseless complaint against me, which was upheld. My career was ruined. I was shattered. My reputation was destroyed. They would not listen to what I had to say. I was guilty before I even came into the room. She came from a wealthy family who had endowed the university. I did not have a chance, I was guilty before I even opened my mouth to defend myself. Ultimately, I was dismissed and removed from the faculty. None of my friends came to my defense. I was shocked, betrayed and ashamed. I swore that I would never talk to them again. I lost my home, my retirement and my good name. I was very angry at first. But, now I am not bitter, because in these latter years I have grown closer to the Master. I enjoy the simplicity of my life." Then looking at his pocket watch he said, "My word, I need to get back to work, I am going to be late." He turned quickly and rushed out the door.

The pastor was stunned by his words, but more so by the gentleness of his sprit and the lack of anger in his voice. The next time he came into the church, the minister told him that he was welcome to pray any time he wanted for as long as he wanted. Over the next few weeks he and the pastor would meet in passing at the door over lunch. The pastor began to look forward to his smile and his presence. Then one week, it occurred to him he might help him by getting him a suit to wear. Maybe he might come to the regular Sunday service. Without telling anyone, he went to the most expensive haberdashery in town and bought the finest suit in the store. He wrapped it in crumpled plain brown paper and tied it with a coarse string. He placed a tag on it with Charles' name on it and left it in the spot that Charles regularly used.

That day the pastor did not come to the sanctuary as he usually did. He went to the choir loft and peered over the balcony to see what would happen when Charles found the package. When he did, Charles opened it slowly and sat there staring at the magnificent suit. He wiped a tear from his eye, gathered up the suit and left, as he had to get back to work. The following day the pastor made like nothing had happened the day before. Charles kind of knew, but said nothing. They greeted each other as they normally did. When it became time to leave Jim said, "It is time to go, thanks" and hurried out the door. He had not ever done that before.

The pastor's heart melted and filled with love. He knew that he had met the Lord there that day. He repeated Charles' prayer form his heart . . . . I came in today to tell you how very happy we have been since we found our friendship and you took away my arrogance. I always love to hear you, I think about you each and every day and so Jesus, this is your pastor checking in on you my friend I love you. Thank you! The following Sunday, Charles came to the regular meeting, but he would only stay for a short time. The pastor understood and was delighted to see him each time he came. They always exchanged a warm glance and deep smile.

The following week, Charles did not come for his normal noon prayer. The pastor was concerned. After several days of missing him, he decided to find out what why Charles was not coming. He missed him and his soft smile. He went to the construction site the following workday to try to find out what had happened. They told him that Charles had fallen ill and was taken to the county hospital and that they thought it had something to do with his blood pressure.

The pastor immediately made his way to the hospital looking for Charles. After at time of fighting his way through the bureaucratic paper work, he located him on the fourth floor indigent ward. He soon discovered the hospital staff was very concerned about his health, but were delighted that he was at the hospital. Apparently somewhere along his life, he picked up the skill of being a clown. Despite the fact that he was in for cardiac observation, he would sneak out into the halls and down to the children's ward. He would pick up the most common of things and with gleeful silliness, bring smiles, giggles and great relief to the children in the cancer ward. Their giggles were his reward and he delighted all of the children.

The next three weeks he was with them, he brought wonderful changes to the ward. He brought smiles, contagious joy and a bit of fun to the children who were so ill. The nurses could not understand how such a jovial man could be so alone. No one brought him cards. No one or ever came to visit him (except the pastor). He never got any calls or gifts or flowers. They just could not understand why no one ever came to visit. Later in the week, the minister voiced the nurses concern that no friends came to visit him.

Looking very surprised, Charles looked at the pastor and said with a winsome smile, "the nurse is wrong, she can't know this but in here with me all the while is my friend whom I visit every day at noon. He sits here at the foot of my bed, he takes my hand when the pain becomes too strong and he leans over to say, I came in today to tell you how very happy we have been since we found our friendship and I took away your arrogance. I always love to hear your prayer, I think about you each and every day and so Charles, this is Jesus checking in on you my friend, I love you. The pastor smiled having learned a great lesson from a clown!

Charles was released from the hospital two weeks later with instructions to find a warmer climate and less physically demanding work. He came one more time to the church to tell the pastor that he had managed to save a bit of money and was moving to Phoenix. In fact he had to catch the bus in just under an hour. The pastor was sad to see him leave but knew that it was the best thing for his health. As they hugged the pastor pushed a $50.00 bill into his coat pocket with his business card saying, please my friend write me when you get settled in Phoenix. They corresponded for many years as only true friends can.

CHAPTER FOUR
New Life

Arise out of the solitude of the cocoon, for a time of renewal. From it will come a new creature, wholly unlike the one that entered the crystals. Upon emergence it is still fragile and will require some time to come to full strength. Once it does, it can stretch our wings, fully alive to rise to a greater growth, as we start the cycle again and again and again.

LONE WOLF AND
THE THREE MUSKETEERS

What a day, it is great time to be alive, and to be young and with spring break coming soon . . . . Who could ask for better. Jim, Mike, Sam and Ted were off for spring break and anticipating one wale of a camping trip to Big Bend. It was going to be fun fun fun!!!! After a hard year hitting the books this was going to be a blast. They had been planning the trip for six months and it was the last great adventure before graduation broke up the three musketeers. They called themselves the three musketeers, despite the obvious fact that there were four of them. Besides as they used to joke, none of them were math majors. They constantly hung around with each other. They were old buddies who originally met in of all places, the Boy Scouts at Camp El Rancho Cima in Wimberley, Texas. At the time Mike was the Trek Director and they worked as Trek leaders, taking scout troops out on the hiking, canoeing trail. All but one of them joined Alpha Phi Omega fraternity at university and continued their long friendship through college. All of them were experienced campers and all loved the majesty of the great doors. All of them were graduating and leaving Texas A&M University for the Real World, except Mike who was going to Oklahoma State to do graduate work. In the back of everyone's minds was the reality of leaving the fun loving college environment for the world of work, responsibility and long days on the freeway. No one welcomed the thought and all were silently lamenting the last days of youth, which were rapidly upon them. Growing up was no fun!

Jim Cornell, is the tallest of them. He towered nearly 6'-4" and was originally from Kansas. He got the nickname, Buckwheat . . . because he was tall, brown on top and from Kansas. Jim majored in civil engineering and had already been interviewing with Linbeck Construction for a REAL job. Jim was as quite as he was tall. He always carefully evaluated every situation, said little then he executed his flawless plan (at whatever he did.) Jim was the natural leader of the group, although none of the other three would admit that.

Ted Doerr, a stocky weight lifter of 5'-6" and 180 pounds of solid muscle, he was pale, complicated and had light dusty haired. He had chosen Forestry as his major. He loved all of nature and had a particular affinity for prairie birds. In fact all the guys regularly kidded him about his end of term project. He did a naturalistic longitudinal study on the Texas Panhandle Prairie Birds taking an inventory of the Quail. He then related the study to the landowners in such a way that they could see how allowing the natural fauna and flora to flourish would make them money (no easy task when cattle is king). Incumbent in the study was taking bird-dropping samples. To determine precisely what they were eating so that he could show that they were not competing with domesticated animals. He was regularly accused of using the taste test to make that determination. This was, as you might guess an allegation he laughed off, but secretly really did not like! To add insult to injury his nickname was DA' DOOR because he was so solid. But it was all in fun.

Sam Betha, is perhaps the most enigmatic of the four. He chose to go to Baylor University as he pursued Sandy, his high school sweetheart. Eventually they would marry and the bachelor party would be a riotous beer filled, blue movie weekend of camping and naked debauchery. Well, that is another story. Sam chose marketing and business and was looking forward to a job with Texas Commerce Bank. Sam is 5'-7", round, brown haired and nearly two hundred pounds of stocky energy. Sam was as you might guess only slightly astray of the Baptist worldview by having the sole distinction, among the musketeers, of being able to chug-a-lug three pictures of beer one after another without barfing. He was the undisputed king of the keg. Sam's nickname was chug-a-lug.

Mike Stewart, is the most boisterous of the gang. He is 5'-9", a scrawny 145 pounds with dusty red brown hair and hazel eyes. Mike was studying environmental design and had the singular distinction in the group of being the poor boy. He was working 3 jobs simultaneously, a WASP, and a C student who as you might guess could not get a scholarship if his life depended on it. He was affectionately, and some times not so affectionately called Mile or More Mike, because when he bellowed, and that was often, he could be heard a mile or more away. He was always talking, making noise or rude sounds, so the nickname really fit him well.

The three musketeers were a tight nit gang of buddies, who had hung together since right after high school. All but Mike was raised in Houston and attended Sharpstown High School. To say that they were old friends is an understatement. They often mused that when one was ready to break wind they all knew it before it happened so that they could sounder up wind!

The plans were made and the goods gathered in short order. Everyone was excited about the trip when they got together on Saturday to load all the junk into the truck. They had decided to use Sam's pickup truck rather than a flock of cars. It would save gasoline and more important it would save money. The well-worn 1970 rust and blue pick-up, with a white cab high camper, was packed to the gills with camping gear and campers. In short order all were packed in the back of the truck. It grunted as it reluctantly accelerated away from the first stop light, riding low on its spring. Sam was at the wheel as they made good time out of town and into the countryside. The trip out of College Station was uneventful as they made their way down HWY 21, the preverbal country road which made its way in not so a straight a path trough the rolling hills of west Texas toward Austin. They got all the way to North Zulch before they had to stop for gasoline and a pit stop. Fifteen minuets on the ground and then it was back on the road. As dusk fell Sam got sleepy and was replaced by Ted who having a pension for lead foot ran the truck almost to the breaking point until they got to the town of Dime Box.

Old Dime Box was a town that time seemed to forget as it was by passed by the railroad earlier in the century. It seemed to all but vanish from the maps, and in fact had been carried away by a tornado in 1922. It was rebuilt the following year as New Dime Box some three-quarters of a mile further down the road. Ted rolled slowly past the remains of the old town and stopped at a Diamond Shamrock gas station for gasoline. By this time the passengers in the back of the truck were restless and no sooner than the truck stopped Sam and Jim decided to throw Mike into the near by creek. Mike objected to being raised out of a sound sleep. A riotous laughing and wrestling match erupted as all three rolled down the creek bed into the water. The gas station attendant did not know quite what to make of this and retreated into the gas station locking the door behind him. It took some 20 minuets of cajoling before he would agree to come out again to sell the motley band enough gasoline to make it to Alice some 250 miles to the south.

Jim switched off with Mike at about 2 a.m. and then Mike with Sam at dawn. The sun was brilliant coming across the high desert country that they had driven into. The azure blue sky was painted brilliant vermilion and iridescent pink as it rose above the horizon. The sparse clouds, like wisps of feathers reflected the brilliant color. The cool of the morning was about to burn off when BLAM, THUMP, THUMP, THUMP! The left rear tire exploded more from lack of tread and than from over weight. Sam responded excellently, by turning sharply into the skid as Mike and Jim bounced uncontrollably in a mix-master of camping gear, coats, boots and dried camping food in the back of the truck. The truck skidded on the shoulder of the road and ran head long into the adjacent ditch. With a thump it bounded up the other side of the ditch and came to a stop as the engine stalled in a cloud of acrid dust and steam. Wide-eyed and stunned Sam blurted out; . . . . Cool lets do that again . . . . Ted's comments were less restrained and much more unprintable.

It took a couple of minuets for Mike and Jim to dig themselves out of the heaps of camping gear and open the door on the camper. The rear camper window was sporting a new crack. Sam surveyed the new crack and made an unprintable comment questioning the ancestry of the ditch. After a few minuets of discussion all agreed that they had been very lucky as the truck could have easily turned over in the ditch. Sam was first to point out what a good driver he and been. This would have normally garnered a spray of catcalls and wise cracks. But in this instance there was meek agreement by all.

Now the task was to get back on the road. The truck had to be unloaded so it could be jacked up in the soft dirt and the new tire put on. All the guys pitched in unloading the truck, which was fortunately not seriously damaged by the skid. There was a new dent in the right front fender and the turning signal lamp cover had been cracked. But all the lights still worked. Sam, however was not pleased to find that the only thing broken in the mix-master in the back of the truck was his bottle of Jim Beam . . . . Boy was he pissed. What are we going to do if a snake bites one of us . . . . He said, to everyone's laughter. After a few minuets all agreed that the reason that the bottle broke was because Mike had hit it with his head in the tumble jumble of the skid. Mike took exception to that, as he would have much rather have drunk it than have to wash it out of the sleeping bag it was wrapped in. He made some off handed comment that he might even start chewing on the sleeping bag so it would not be wasted. Everyone half believed that he would.

Everyone pitched in unloading the truck. It seemed that the amount and volume of stuff in the back of the truck had increased four fold. With a little grumbling and a few rude comments it was unloaded in about 15 minuets. Sam took on the job of removing the tire. He unscrewed the spare from under the truck bed. The spare was only marginally less threadbare than the tire that had blown. The truck was jacked up, the tire replaced and back on the ground in a few minuets. The skid had bent the rim on the blown tire and Sam wanted to dump it in the ditch. Ted, objected to that plan, as he was more ecologically aware than the rest of them. After several minuets of wise cracks and then several more of discussions old Boy Scout Training finally won out as the useless tire and wheel were hoisted back up under the truck and bolted down. The only consolation was that all agreed that Ted should reload the truck, which he agreed to do. After five minuets of sarcastic directions on how to do it properly, a particularly nasty look from Ted and a couple of belches from Sam everyone pitched in to reload the truck. In short order everything was on board and they were back on the road again.

By this time it was about lunch and it was getting very hot. The countryside had changed from plateau to arid high Mexican desert. About noon they turned south at Alice and made for the boarder. The road was straight as an arrow with nothing breaking the horizon but a line of telephone poles, a few cactus and lots of HOT. The heat of the day was shimmering up in mirages. BANZI!!!!!!, Sam screamed as he barreled down the newly paved road. An occasional buzzard on the phone line and a lizard or two was all that they saw for the next 118 miles. Buy this time everyone, except Sam was getting very hungry, or so it seems. Jim tried to cajole him into stopping, which he resisted, wanting to make the Rio Grand by sunset. At Jim's instigation and after some lip reading of the words, Pound on the Truck, through the rear window! Mike and Ted started pounding and rocking back and forth in the bed of the truck. That convinced Sam to stop for lunch.

He picked the small town of Hidalgo, just 15 miles from the Mexican Boarder. This place was so small that it did not even have a post office and the main street was not paved. He pulled off into the gravel parking lot of The Sanchez Diner. To amplify his annoyance he waited until the last minute before he turned. That caused everyone to slam against each other as he fishtailed into the parking lot and stopped in a cloud of dust. Sam thought it was hilarious, although he was the only one. The restaurant was little more than a hole in the wall, and well worn with age. It was a dilapidated wood building with peeling paint and cracked boards. There were five small tables with tattered faded red and white-checkered tablecloths. The seats were wood with wicker in fill, some of which had a perceptible bulge where more than one abundant customer had left their impression. The bar looked a hundred years old, with chips and dings from countless cowboy belt buckles. In the corner was a booth that would handily seat five. Mike immediately made a dash for the toilet. While he was indisposed Sam hatched a plan for a joke with the other guys. When Mike came out of the toilet all the guys were waiting patiently to be seated, despite the sign that said "please seat yourselves". Sam made his way for the booth, making sure that Mike was in the middle blocked in on both sides. He had conspired to play a trick on Mike who was the only Yankee in the group. He was going to show Mike a little about the wonderful Tex-Mex cuisine. Mike unknowingly slipped into the center of the booth and did not have a clue what was about to happen to him.

Everyone settled in to read the menu. The waiter brought a large basket of fried chips and hot sauce. After a few munches and a couple of minuets of intense reading Sam smiled broadly. "Ja-lap-anoss, Ja-lap-an-ossss" Sam said! Mike was reared in the North and came to Texas from California to go to university. So he did not know what a Jalapeno was. "Yeah, Ja-lap-an-ossssss" he said, "they are sweet Mexican pickles, you are going to love them." Mike was a bit skeptical, but simultaneously everyone chimed in., "oh yeah, they are good . . . you are going to love them." Being a bit wiser than the average bear Mike insisted that someone show him how good they were. When the waiter greeted the gang at the table the second time, the trap has already been set. The plan was falling nicely into place as Mike was firmly locked into the center of the corner booth and blocked in by Ted and Jim, one on each side of him. The enchilada special for everyone was the order. Ice tea all around, and oh by the way a side order of Ja-lap-an-oss . . . the waiter hesitated a moment then he remembered their agreement. Hot flower tortillas, ice tea and enchiladas appeared in short order. Jim volunteered to take the first bite of the sweet pickles, readily flushing. Sam, asking Ted a nonsense question about the camping site to distract Mike. In the mean time Jim quickly spat out the Jalapenos into his napkin and drank a quick gulp of tea. Jim then said, "UMMMM good, Mike you are going to love them, and be sure to chew up the seeds that is where the real sweet part is."

Mike reluctantly took a nibble out of the Jalapeno handed to him, and it was a real big beefy one . . . . Sam said, "good grief Mike, take a real bite", and shoved his hand against Mike's so that it force virtually the entire pepper into his mouth. Mike chomped down and immediately, wide-eyed spat it out to the riotous laughter of all the musketeers. It was like having napalm dropped in your mouth on a hot summer day. It burned everything from the tongue up with a raging wild fire. Panic-stricken Mike reached for the water. Jim pushed it to the other side of the table. Mike reached for the tea and Sam gave it to Ted. Mike reached for the sugar and it was quickly pushed away. Mike tried to get up and Sam and Jim both pushed him down by the top of the shoulders. All were having great fun, except Mike, who began to tear. He blurted out," Cowabunga, if someone don't let give me some water I am going to walk across this table and make a run for the toilet." Everyone reared back and roared again with laughter. That was just the thing Mike needed as they loosened their grips slightly. He leapt up, placing one foot in the tortillas the second in the enchiladas and the third step he hit the floor at a dead run for the toilet.

After a few minuets Mike returned, very flushed and sat down at the end of the booth, where he could get away. The laughter had subsided, and a fresh dish of enchiladas had appeared, to the sheepish grins of all around. The waiter, still snickering, handed Mike a cool glass of buttermilk that finally quenched the fire. Mike looked sternly at all his buddies and said, "Vengeance is mine sayth the cook." The impact of which was lost on all, at the time, in the continued laughter at the success of the joke. They had forgotten that Mike was the cook, for the first half of the trip . . . and he would have his revenge. After having had a good laugh all around and finishing their lunch everyone piled back into the beat up old red truck and headed South again.

This spring was unseasonably hot and the day rapidly became unbearable. Fortunately for the guys in the front they had a tepid air conditioner to cool them ever so slightly. As for the two in the back, it was only slightly above bearable as long as the truck was moving and the wind was blowing through the open side windows. The countryside around Alice and along much of the border offers little for the eye, especially on a very hot summer day. By midmorning it was 115. There was little relief from the intense sun, except to keep moving down the long straight black road. Sam wanted to pull off and let the old truck rest for a while, as it was starting to over heat, but that thought was quickly abandoned when everyone objected. The compromise was to turn off the air conditioner (so as to not stress the engine) and to press on until dusk.

We stopped for a stretch break about two hours later. Immediately everyone headed for the bushes, to uh relieve the pain so to speak. After recycling the tea from lunch everyone was in a better mood. Then it was back to the truck and on the road again. Sometime around 2 am Jim took a wrong turn. Instead of turning to the south he managed to end up going north. So in the early the next morning we found ourselves nearly out of gasoline and 65 miles off course in the wrong direction. Sam was not amused. He made it infinitely clear that some folks can not tell their directions from a hole in the ground, although it was not quite worded that way . . . . any way you get the drift. Checking the map, we determined that the nearest town was Terlingwa, and judging from the surrounding desert, probably with a total population of two. We had no choice, we were nearly out of gas and we had to try to find a gas station fast. When we drove into Terlingwa our hearts sunk. It was a ghost town. I mean a real ghost town, it appeared that no one had lived there for fifty years. Jim took the Texas High Way Department magazine out of the glove box and looked it up. There was a small article in it about the Chili cook off that happened there every September. But this was not September, and although there were supposed to be 800 people there then. There was no one and certainly no gas station. He went on to read how this had been a town of 4500 people around WW2 when quick silver was found there, and that when it petered out in the early 1950's everyone had moved away.

We all decided to explore, after all how often do you get to go through a real ghost town. By this time the entire town consisted of half a dozen dilapidated wooden buildings and, fifty or so bare foundations and what appeared to be a burned out brick building on the hill. It was sad, in a way, but the entire site was covered with tons of litter, paper, boxes, cans and just plain trash. Apparently the chili cook off folks were not the neatest people in the word. We split up and began to explore around the old town. I made for the brick building on the hill. It was an old school house and apparently it had some time ago been involved in a fire. The hike up the hill was simple. I had to side step a scorpion but other than that not much else to report. I surveyed the building to get a better view of what it had been. The bricks were covered with black soot and were blistered. The walls were half collapsed. You could see the black burn marks on the timbers that had fallen into the main room. On the gnarled pressed metal ceiling that had collapsed into one of the classrooms there was still a little yellow paint mixed among the soot and rust. As I was maneuvering to take a shot of the Devils Post Pile Peak through a stark gray sun bleached wooden widow frame (without panes) I hesitated. This was truly a Kodak Moment . . . . I heard a gravely voice say . . . "hey!!! you bubba what the hell you doin' here?"

I turned around to see a scruffy 80ish looking toothless cowboy waving a six-shooter over his head in a menacing manner. He demanded, "get the hell out of here bubba." My eyes widened and I said, "UH . . . . , Sir I was just taking a picture and uh we almost ran out of gas and well uh, sir . . . yes you bet I will be glad to leave." I made my way quickly back down the hill toward the truck with the old codger not far behind me. Fortunately he had holstered his gun and was just being sure that I would leave as I said I would. I found Ted dropping rocks into the deep main mineshaft and I hollered at him to get the other guys we need to leave now! A few moments later Sam and Jim came around the corner of an adjacent building. The old codger drew his pistol again and pointed it at them. They stopped short in their tracks wide eyed.

There for a moment it looked very tense. Then Jim in his slow lanky voice said, "sir, we are old Boy Scouts, who took a wrong turn and are looking for gasoline." That seemed to break the ice as the old codger, lowered his pistol aiming it at the ground. Then he remarked that he had been an Eagle Scout long time ago. They chatted for a moment and then the old man, introduced himself as Bill. He volunteered to take us to the nearest gas station (some 22 miles away) at Prickly Pair Point. We were grateful as this town was not even on the map and we had little gasoline to spare. When we arrived there we were surprised to find that it was not a town after all, but a brand new Fina truck stop with all the frills. We gladly filled up with cheep gasoline and cold soda. Bill was glad to have the company as he was the only resident of Terlingwa (except for two stray dogs). He was employed by the Peabody Mining Company, who owned the land, to guard it so that no one fell down the 356-foot deep main shaft (or so he measured it by timing the fall of the stone.) Apparently from talking with him he was born in the town and was the last of the real men who stayed, since Running Bear, his sidekick had died the previous winter.

We drove him back to Terlingwa and were invited to stay for supper. Being as it was early evening, we knew the chances of getting lost again in the dark were very good, we agreed to stay. He was delighted to have the company. But we made it clear that we had to be off the next morning as we were to meet the Trek leader at the Big Bend Main Ranger Station. He understood and led us to his shanty. He lived in a dilapidated wood and dirt walled enclosure in what appeared to be the opening of a closed mine. The dirt floor was no surprise, but the TV was. I remarked about it and Bill said, don't worry as it did not work any way and he was low on gasoline for the generator. Besides he said, "I did not miss the noise at all since he could only get mostly the Mexican stations anyhow."

As night fell he brewed up some strong coffee. The pot he used looked like it had not been cleaned in 20 years. I was not sure weather the cup was any better or not. It was either many months of unwashed coffee stains, or I did not want to know. But the coffee was hot and the night had taken on a bit of a chill. We sat in front of his make shift home talking about the country and the old times. After a while he disappeared into the house one time to retrieve some old newspaper clippings from WW2. Apparently he had been one of the few survivors from the initial marine assault force that hit Iwo Jima. He had been awarded the Bronze Star and had a metal plate in his head due to the battle injuries he received that day. He said that they said that he was not all quite there after that, as he chuckled and patted his pistol with a sly grin that sent chills down our spines. That gesture was intended to make us a bit nervous . . . and it did. He grinned broadly as he looked each one of us in the eye!!!

As the night wore on it got cooler and the coffee tasted much better. After a time the talk turned to our trip, of which Ted was more happy than to share our plans to hike and camp for a week. The plan was to end the trip at Indian Springs on top of the East Rim. The moment Ted mentioned Indian Springs the old codger got wide eyed. His expression was exaggerated in the flickering firelight. It made us wonder enough to ask what was wrong. To our surprise he remarked, "Don't you know that place is haunted!!!!!" Of course we didn't know, nor did we believe it. But figuring it was a good night for a ghost story we played along.

Bill related the story of the local legend. So it happened in 1881 or was it 1887, well no matter it was true, he swore. This was a time when the old west was fast fading away and the machines of the 20th century were making their debut on the landscape. Trains had for some time plied their way across the prairie and in their wake, planted towns and farms and villages. The first victim of the infernal machines were the buffalo. These mighty beast were the mainstay of the Arapaho and Apache who for many years had wandered these mountains. The buffalo was both clothing, house and food. Every part of the beast was used. The bones made the ribs of the roundhouses, its hides made up the roof, walls, and floor. Its meat fed the people and kept them content in the cold winters when it was mixed into dried pemmican. The buffalo was beast, friend and brother to the Indian. It was critical to their survival and without it they would parish. The train, the buffalo gun and all the infernal machines of the coming new century had driven all but a few of the herds to the north nearly into extinction.

The last remaining small herd of buffalo managed to survive on the East Rim Bluff. Apparently there was sufficient bunch grass and water at the spring to maintain the small herd of 60 or so. The Indians knew of the herd. They kept it secret fearing for the starvation of their children. Late in the fall of that year a buffalo hunter, by the name of James Cromwell and his three companions, Micah O'tool, Theodore Griffin and Samson Ward wandered into the country in search of hides. They found the pickings very thin as by this time of the year most of the remaining buffalo had moved further north for better fodder. They knew the salt grass was tall along the Rio Grand this time of the year and they had hope that they might catch a few stray buffalo and make a couple of dollars. Their search of the Rio Grand Valley was fruitless, and besides it had been taken over by long horn cattle and barbed wire. All of whom belonged to someone. "*X*#XXX!!!!!", Theodore was known to say, "the city slickers are taking over the country, pretty soon there won't be any open range left". In fact every time he came across a barbed wire fence he made a practice of cutting the wire, just for spite. Our unsavory group made their way up the valley, to somewhere where the bluffs begun to raise out of the desert, but no one is quite sure exactly where that was. But it was somewhere near here. As the story is told, they ran across a drunkard Kyowa who hated the Arapaho, in town who, for a bottle of red eye told them the story of the lost herd that stayed year round on top of the East Rim.

They went to the assay office to locate a map of the area. They made their way toward the rim the following morning. Now the East Rim is not just a freestanding bluff. It is only the eastern part of a massive mesa, which rose out of the desert plains like a great 50-mile long 35-mile wide table, 500-600 feet off the desert floor. The East Rim, as the name suggest faces to the east. In fact it is told that you could see Kansas City from there on a clear day (or so they said.)

The buffalo hunters made several attempts to scale the bluff with out much success. They were about to give up when Theodore saw a wild mountain ass working its way up the side of the mesa on a crooked path. He almost missed it as whenever it felt it was being watched it would stand still. Its gray coat blended in perfectly with the broken stone of the bluff. If it had not knocked some rocks loose that tumbled down the hillside he would not have seen the ass at all. He watched if for a few moments when it disappeared behind a clump of cedar trees then reappeared some 150 feet further up the bluff. Apparently there was a hidden trail up there. With some difficulty the buffalo hunters made their way to the top of the bluff. Much to their surprise the top of the mesa was lush in tall bunch grass. The trees were small owing to the altitude and the ones at the edge of the bluff were growing nearly horizontal to the ground because of the constant wind coming up over the edge.

They made their way in a serpentine search pattern from south to north looking for the buffalo. They found some bones, a skull or two, some dried prairie apples but not much more. At the evening of the third day they spotted a small wisp of smoke coming from the horizon to the north. Fearing hostile Indians they waited until dusk and quietly made their way toward the smoke. When they came upon a gully near the Indian springs they worked their way quietly up the gully until they where within in eyeshot of the camp. There they found three small hide and bone roundhouses. Standing near by were horses tied to a line between two trees and four braves. Behind the roundhouses were stretching frames with fresh hides staked to the ground for drying. They crept closer to the camp until they could see the four braves seated around a fire cooking meat on a forked stick. Silently the buffalo hunters simultaneously raised their rifles. When Theodore nodded they all fired. The first Indian was thrown back against the roundhouse with such force that it collapsed on top of him. The brave sitting to his immediate right was thrown across the fire extinguishing it. The third brave's head was split open like a ripe melon, splattering the pile of hides next to him. The last brave was struck in the chest just left of his right arm but managed to struggle off into the high grass. The buffalo hunters leapt up, and gave a blood curling war cry as they pursued the fourth brave. The brave made a valiant effort to defend himself, despite his one immobilized arm. In fact it is told that he managed to bury his knife to the hilt in the leg of one of his assailants before they bashed his brains out with the butt of their guns.

Our brave buffalo hunters returned to the camp to claim their prizes. The ate the meat already cooked and began to pick through the hides. Micah went back to their camp to get the packhorses as James searched the other round house. Inside he found a squaw holding a male papoose. He raised the butt of his gun to crush her skull when the baby began to cry. In that split second, a small bit of humanity rushed to his mind and he retained. He just could not harm the baby, so he motioned with the barrel of his rifle for her to go. She quickly picked up the child and disappeared into the darkness. Theodore had returned by this time and heard the ruckus. Micah raised his rifle to his shoulder and fired twice over their heads as they fled. Then he bragged how he had blasted the no good Indian squaw on the run, fully knowing that he had missed her as she was well out of range when he fired.

Early the next morning the hunters made their way to the lost trail, to return to the valley and sell the hides. They got a late morning start, or so it is told. When they got half way down the trail the long shadows of late afternoon had fallen obscuring the trail. They rode back and forth most of the rest of the day trying to find the way down the bluff. As dusk fell they made a fatal error and turned down a dead end canyon. No one quite knows what happened that night, but some years later the bones of men and their horses were found at the end of that canyon. They say that there was a landslide that knocked them off the trail to their death, others say that some more Indians attacked them, but I believe that the ghost of them Indians that had their revenge . . . . Fact bein', it is said that the spirits of them Indians wander the east rim lookin' for revenge, so that they might one day enter the happy hunting ground . . . who know . . . who knows . . ." He ended the story with a wide toothless grin. Sam took a deep sigh, that broke the silence and we all laughed nervously then called it a night.

The next morning we were up early. We thanked our host for his hospitality, rolled up our sleeping bags, packed the truck and headed out for the Base Camp. About 4 p.m. the truckload of campers turned west-southwest toward the Rio Grand Valley. The vegetation was much more abundant there owing to the river water and springs in the area. It even cooled just a bit. Everyone was thankful for that. We were out of the desert, at least for a while. We drove until dusk before pulling off at a roadside park to rest for the evening meal. It was Budweiser all around, and cold cuts from the cooler. The bread was a bit soggy on the end, owing to an unfortunate up set during the blown tire incident. But other than that, we had to eat it all as the ice was almost gone. A six-pack and a couple of belches later we were on our way again.

Jim and Sam alternated driving all night long. When we awoke the next morning it was to a glorious sight of royal pink sky and light purple sunlight peaking over the edge of the base camp at Big Bend National Park. It was an incredible sight. The Pinion pines were little more than 4 feet tall because of the low water level and acid in the soil. They were sparsely scattered along the rim and a bit more thick toward the valley of the caldera. The spring was still running and you could hear the sound of the waterfall down the valley as it cascaded to the desert floor below.

We parked adjacent to the park ranger's office and waited. Apparently 5am was only a few hours too early for the ranger to get up. After a moment we noticed a portly man on a moped zip buy us with a small chain saw on the back. He puttered down the road and cut off across an open field spitting up dust and rocks as he went. After a few moments we heard the sound of the saw. Then he returned triumphantly with a green pinion dragging behind his moped on a nylon rope. We were all speechless as we knew that cutting wood in this arid climate was strictly forbidden. It was not a few minuets later when the man returned in tow by a park ranger. He definitely was not a happy camper. We found out later that he was fined $1,500, with his moped and saw both being confiscated. What a twit, Ted remarked, anyone should know better than to cut a green tree for firewood, and especially here in the desert . . . . A few moments later, Mr. Twit drove by in his Winnebago, apparently encouraged to leave the park by the ranger as well. "New Jersey licenses plates . . . ." Ted remarked, "Why am I not surprised."

Shortly after that, the park ranger's office opened and we went inside to meet our guide, Lone Wolf. He was an Arapaho Indian, who had taken treks through these mountains for 35 years. He was the founder and owner of Buffalo Excursions Inc. Ted had heard about him from some buddies in the Forestry Department. Ted had made all the arrangements, including the hard part, collecting the money. We were to meet our guide at the park and go from there to the river, raft down the Rio Grand. Then we were to hike to The Pinnacles and finish up on the top of the East Rim. The only problem was that Lone Wolf was not there! After a few moments of confusion, we decided to check the registered itineraries. But that could not be done until the next day when the head ranger, Ranger Warner got back from official business in El Paso. So we set out for a camping spot in the basin. It only took a few minuets for us to find a spot, pitch our tents, and decide to hike to the waterfalls. Although it was hot it was a very pretty day.

It was a beautiful day for a day trip, cotton candy cumulus clouds hung at irregular intervals across the sky, casting wonderfully cool shadows across the base camp. The wind had picked up a bit and it was very pleasant to feel the cool breeze on our foreheads as we started our Trek. Sam was in the lead and Jim bringing up the rear (as his stride was so big that we had to run to keep up with him.) We wound our way down the red earth path and through the Juniper trees, until we could hear the gurgle of moving water. We found the creek in a clump of willow bushes and plunged our hands into the remarkably cold water. It was incredibly refreshing as opposed to the warmth of the day. A small Brooke trout darted back and forth from bank to bank, seeking shelter under the overhanging grass. I dipped my hands into the water to take a drink when I heard a rustle in the brush to my right. I glanced over my shoulder and saw what appeared to be the silhouette of an old man, and then it was gone. Sam, "I said, did you see that"? "UH, there was something, but I could not quite tell what it was". The both of us thought a moment, perplexed and then agreed that it might have been a small deer. "AH, don't worry about that," he said and we proceeded down the trail.

The trail snaked its way for 2 ½ more miles, slowly rising toward the cut in the caldera wall. I could see the incredible contrast of the red sandstone framing the brilliant blue sky beyond. Just up ahead through a gently rising V shape in the canyon wall we could see the valley far below us in the hazy distance. We could hear the sound of the waterfall echoing against the stone. By this time we were close enough to the edge of the caldera wall to be in the afternoon shadow. It was wonderfully cool and the wind picked up as it whistled through the notch in the canyon wall. The creek ended in a large pool of crystal—light greenish water. It was incredible. The only thing to do was to go for a swim. Skinny-dipping was the instant response. There were cute and not so cute wise cracks, born of young virile libidos that followed disrobing. Not withstanding the water was extremely cold, cold enough to make your manhood pucker. We all dove in. Once past the shock of the difference in the air and water temperature it was incredible. We all had a wonderful time swimming for an hour and a half or so. Then it was time to eat. Mike hollered, break out the Bernard's Freeze Dried Food as he had already sun dried himself (al la natural) on the rocky beach. Much to everyone's delight he also managed to get sun burned in a couple of very tender places. This as you might guess was the brunt of many wise cracks as the trip wore on. Jim was already out of the water and into the packs for the dried food. It took a few minutes of soaking for the dehydrated peaches to look anything like what they were advertised to be. But once reconstituted they were wonderful. Hard tack, jelly and peanut butter squeezed from an aluminum foil package and the ever popular green goop (lime Kool-Aid) were the fare of the day.

There were a few moments for pictures and then it was time to return to camp. Ted, as was his custom, always ventured too close to the edge of the precipice. He insisted that he had to get a photograph of the bottom of the waterfall, from the top. Now this was impossible as the water evaporated before hit his the valley floor some 550 feet below. But that was Ted. He eked his way to the slippery edge of the waterfall and shot down into the valley floor with his camera. The only person who was not nervous about the whole affair was Ted. But he was a little nuts anyway.

The trip back up the river, took about an hour and a half. The sun was setting fast in the caldaria and we could already see the morning star and a faint wisp of a half moon by the time we made the crest of the hill looking down on the base camp. Sam and I could not help but think about the deer that we thought we had seen and then did not . . . . The only rustle in the bushes we saw on the way back turned out to be an armadillo, who in its haste had run headlong into a rock, being even more afraid of us than we of it. It regained it's footing in a split second and disappeared into the underbrush in a thunder of crackling sounds. We decided to stop and cook dinner. We selected a wide bare spot in the trail that obviously had been used as a campsite before. Sam reassembled the scattered campfire stones. It was Mike's turn to cook dinner. And what a fare. Beef Stroganoff, corn bread, vanilla pudding, and beans. Mike was an incredible cook on an open fire. But he could not boil water without burning it on a kitchen stove. But on an open fire he was a master chef. Everyone else settled into the trailside camp spot, as Mike got the dinner together. Ted went for water, and Sam and Jim scourged for small bits of squaw wood. After a few moments everyone returned having accomplished their tasks. Sam was still thinking about the rustling in the woods and the shadow he saw, when Mike spooned up a heaping spoon of blue stroganoff onto his tin plate. Somewhat startled by the color he hesitated to the snickers of the others. Ted, began to make a wise crack when Mike held up the bottle of iodine water purification tablets, that Ted had given him. We all knew that iodine would do that to the starch in the noodles and it was OK to eat. After all had eaten their fill, it was noticed that Mike did not eat any of the blue vanilla pudding (and there was none left to be had.) Only Sam made a remark about it but no one else noticed.

After a few moments, Rising slowly, grinning broadly he announced, "Whoa to yeeee who pissith off the cook . . . vengeance is mine sayith the cook" . . . holding up an empty bag of TETROX (strong camp soap used to coat the bottom of the pots so that the soot would wash off easily). Everyone knew what that meant . . . super tots for a week that not even Kopectate could fix. In an instant there was a tumble of elbows and armpits as everyone rushed Mike at one time, rolling and laughing, kicking, and tumbling across the open ground, into the bushes and into the creek. After a few minuets the laughter subsided, Sam got serious and asked, did you really put Tetrox in the pudding . . . . Mike reluctantly admitted, NO. But he warned them never to put Jal-ap-in-oooos on his plate again. Everyone agreed!.

At dusk when we made it back to base camp it was as though the whole place had been transformed. When we left there were fewer than a dozen campers in the whole 150-acre site. When we got back there must have been 200 camping groups there. Unknown to us while we were at the falls a Winnebago club had arrived from of all places NEW YORK CITY. There were enough Winnebago's parked in the caldera now to pay off half of the national debt. It was like mini-suburbia all over again. Man, what a bummer, this is what we were trying to get away from, but we were stuck, until we could get to the ranger station the following morning.

That night about 10:30 another Winnebago drove up, this one was a 50 footer. Apparently it was a straggler. It was the biggest darn one I had ever seen. An elderly couple sundered out of it when it stopped not 15 feet from our tent. They rolled out a canopy and set the leveling feet. Then the old man cranked up his generator. Capow, Capow, Capow, (apparently having a defective muffler) it chugged and echoed through the caldaria, much to the distaste of everyone. After about an hour of watching TV and eating their dinner they turned out the lights and turned on the air conditioner and went to bed. It was 2 am. No one in the entire camp could have possibly gotten any sleep before then as the noise was so loud. Everyone including our group were very happy that he had turned that darn generator off. We only wished that he had done it much earlier. At 7am the next morning we were greeted by the elderly gentleman asking if we had seen anyone messing with his generator last night. It seems that the spark plug wire was missing and the generator would not run without it. No one had seen or heard anything. So on he went to the next camp not particularly happy looking for an answer.

When 8 o'clock came around we made it to the ranger station. We asked for the ranger. We were told that he had been delayed in El Paso and would not return for three more days. We discussed the situation and finally came to the conclusion that, since we were late, that Lone Wolf had gone ahead of us to set up our base camp on the East Rim. This is not what we thought we had planned for, but as we were all experienced campers we had a good US geodetic survey map and a good compass so after a few moments we agreed to start the Trek. We thanked the ranger, notified him of our plans on his registry and went back to the truck. As we drove back down the road and out the valley entrance we passed the Winnebago that had been such a noise polluter the night before. I noticed the missing spark plug wire dangling in the wind from the driver's side mirror frame. I blurted out, "Sam look a that", he glanced over his shoulder and gave back a broad Cheshire cat grin. Nothing more needed to be said . . . silence is golden especially in the wilderness. We drove off toward the East Rim.

The East Rim could not be reached by any truck. It was completely isolated which is exactly why we wanted to go there. They say that the view is incredible from there is an understatement of the highest order. We knew that it is local legend that the spring at the top was haunted. I was intrigued by the entire idea. The hike up the mesa was difficult. You had to gain more than 500 feet elevation to get to the top. But to accomplish that you had to hike more than 15 3/4 miles of switchbacks after we parked the truck. Lugging all our junk was no easy trick. By the time we got started boy oh boy we all had wished that we had packed lighter. The base of the valley was hot, dry Mexican Desert. And I mean HOT. Nearly hot enough to repent, but not quite! The only ones who liked it there were the scorpions and the prairie rattlers. We all made haste to load up, lock the truck and make for the trail. Finally we were on our way!

The trail followed the Rio Grand for a while. This was in stark contrast to the desert we had just driven through. The strata of the rock were inclined to the surface of the water, making it appear that the water was running up hill. In many places the trail was little more than a few inches wide as we clung to the red stonewalls of the canyon. The wind had carved remarkable pinnacles and shapes in the soft stone. The edge of the mesa had been transformed into a series of slender freestanding spires several hundred feet tall and only ten or twelve feet wide. It was remarkable. The banded stone stood in stark contrast to the powder blue sky silhouetted against it. The wind could be heard to blow hauntingly through the narrow channels between the pencils. As we walked up the hill we could hear our own footsteps echoing against the ever-narrowing walls. We made our way up a slue and then took a couple of switchbacks when Sam pointed up ahead and a silhouette of a figure staging on one on the pencil's. It looked like an old Indian man . . . or so I thought but the consensus was that it must have been a free form mountain climber, or how else could anyone make it to the top of the 200 foot tall 10 wide pinnacle without any gear. While everyone put on a brave face, everyone secretly had some doubt, because as the shadow from the sun shifted from light to dark he seemed to simply disappear . . . . The howl of the wind in between the pinnacles sounded like a low slow eerie growl. But it also seemed rhythmic, almost like an ancient Indian chant. It gave all of us goose bumps! We picked up our packs and our pace as we resumed our Trek up the Rim. The trails are fairly well marked and it was easy to find the way up. After all it was the only way to go, up I mean.

The trail began to work its way along the other side of a slight rise as it turned sharp to the left. There we got a good glimpse of the Rio Grand, not much more that a few feet across at this point. By this time we were hot, tired and dirty. Any body of water would have been welcomed. In a heartbeat, we were stripped to the shorts, leaving packs, boots, pants and shirts strung in a chaotic line between the rise and the water. Splashing one after another we fell into the shallow rocky water (not more than a foot deep). And cold, it was cold enough to freeze your do da blue. What a shock, this far south, in the middle of the desert and water cold as ice. After a few minuets, the yelping subsided and no one complained. The coolness of the water was very welcome in the 100 plus degree heat. We all languished there for a while, then we heard the sound of a falling rock. Everyone stopped and searched with their eyes. Seeing nothing we continued with our frolicking. After a few moments we found a deeper hole in the river and were able to actually swim. It was wonderful, clear, cool and calm. Then we heard a small cascade of falling rocks again. Instinctively everyone froze expecting a rockslide or something. Once again nothing could be seen. Then a third time after about 15 minutes later another small rock cascaded down the side of the mountain. All our hearts were in our throats. What the heck could it be we thought. Then Ted pointed up the hill on the Mexican side of the border and laughed . . . saying, "look at that." It was a small gray burrow colt carefully picking its way across the slate slag of a long ago mountain slide. It was really quite incredible as the burrow seemed to have glue on its feet. The slope of the slag was easily 50 degrees and he seemed to be walking as though he was on the valley floor, only occasionally dislodging a loose rock. The burrow was nearly the same color as the stone so he was very difficult to see. If it had not been for the glint of the sun off his eye no one would have seen him. "A bit nervous are we" came from Jim after a moment of tense silence. It was just enough to break the ice and we all yucked it off. But in the back of our minds we were all still a bit nervous about the shadows we had seen and the odd sound on the wind.

Along about 2:30 PM we gathered our scattered belongings and started a Bernard's Special Dry Lunch, dry peaches (not hydrated), hard tack, jelly, peanut butter and green goop. Not the best of lunches but filling and quick. We wanted to make the East Rim by nightfall. Sam wolfed down the last cracker and we were on our way (Sam always had room for more crackers—what a sick boy!!!!!) After about half an hour the trail meandered away from the river and out into the desert. By this time we could see the East Rim looming on the horizon down upon us. This part of the trail snaked its way across the hard pan of the desert floor, and at the hottest time of the day. Talk about rotten luck. We were not looking forward to being sweat hogs. But there was no choice. If we waited any longer it would be well after dark before we got to the Rim. It would be foolish at best to try to scale the Rim on a trail we did not know after the sun set. So we all struck out across the desert toward the Rim, which we could clearly see some 6 miles in the distance. The closer we got to the Rim the longer the trail seemed to get. We walked for three hours over rolling hills and through gullies on what we thought was a straight shot turned into the lost trail. Then the trail turned sharply South and started to parallel the edge of the rim. Fortunately, much of it fell in the shadows as we were well into the afternoon and walking along the base of the East Rim was much cooler than out on the hard pan of the desert. It was much cooler there and the vegetation was more abundant as the morning dew stayed longer on the east than at the rest of the valley floor edge of the mesa. There were even a few wild pepper trees interspersed among the Yucca and the Piotie Cactus. But mostly it was scrub brush, creosote and prickly pare. Not much of a welcoming mix. But to my surprise we saw rabbit, deer and fox droppings along the trail, so it seemed that despite the hot climate and sacristy of water there was a healthy mix of animals.

As the slope of the trail began to increase we noticed a silhouette on the adjacent ridge by the glint of sunlight off field glasses. It was not much more than thirty minutes when we rounded a bend we found a park ranger waiting for us. We were surprised to find out that he was watching for longhairs picking the Piotie buds. It was a protected plant, the buds were after all a spring thing and well if you smoked it was certainly a hallucinogenic. Fortunately we were only interested in the dry branches, which made excellent bola ties for handkerchiefs. He skeptically accepted our explanation, did not confiscate the stalks we had collected as they were obviously long ago dead. Plus not having seen us pluck any buds he could not make a case. He let us go on our way with a warning that to violate this law meant a $5,000 fine and or 10-20 years in prison. We acknowledged his warning, assured him we were old Boy Scouts who would never do such a stupid thing and went on our way (but not without some rude mutterings about bureaucrats.)

Shortly the trail turned steeply upward. All of us, young or not huffed and puffed under the weight of our packs and the steep climb. The trail was not easy to follow. In several places it simply disappeared. Except for the tracks of what appeared to be a small burrow to follow across the less traveled spots we might have gotten totally lost. It took the rest of the day to make it to the top of the Rim. Buy that time we were nearly out of water, at the end of our energy and ready for a rest. Ted was the last one up the hill, having stopped to watch some quail. By the time he got to the top the rest of us were ready to press on to the spring. Needless to say he was not as enthusiastic as the rest of us. So we waited for him to regain his strength. Fortunately he had also stopped to make some drinking water out of a sinkhole. He carefully screened out the green algae slime to produce a wonderful dark gray water, which he impregnated with iodine tablets. It must have taken him half an hour to produce two canteens of water, that as you might expect tasted of strong iodine, ironically it was only a short hike to the clear water of the spring. We did not have the heart to tease him about it or tell him that we had already found and used the spring. His heart was in the right place.

As we sat at the edge of the East Rim, I could see how they thought you might be able to see Kansas City form there. We were at the height of a wide arc in the ridge that extended a full quarter of a mile out into the valley beyond the rest of the mesa. You could see from due north to the New Mexican border to the Southwest in one grand panorama. You could see the green snaking line of the Rio Grande as it meandered down form the Chico Mountains. Beyond that, somewhat obscured by the haze was Old Mexico. Farther to the Southeast was Texas as far as the eye could see. Scattered like miniature dark feathers helter—skelter along the horizon were small thunderstorms, giving their lifeblood of water to the desert. Beyond them was a massive gray and white wall of clouds from a front making its way across the panorama. Patches of green could be seen below that where farms, and the shadows of the cloud on the hills were all intermingled. To the direct East was the makings of a dust storm, which obscured what was beyond it in a powder brown haze. To the north we thought we could see Terlingwa and the lights of the Fina Gas station. But that was probably more fanciful imagination than anything else. One thing was for certain, this was one of the most spectacular sights I had ever seen. It took 11 photographs in sequence north to south to get it all in. They were going to be impossible to match as the clouds would move faster than the pictures could be taken. But I did not care as it was so spectacular. This was truly God's Country. After a moment I had the strange feeling that someone was watching me. I turned around and got a glance of a ghostly male figure standing behind me in the shadow of trees. Then the wind picked up a bit, howling in a menacing manner. It had the strange characteristic of sounding like a faint Indian chant as it echoed against the Rim. When I walked over to the trees, there was no one there. The hair stood up on the back of my neck again. I mentioned it later to Ted, who was near me at the time and he reluctantly admitted that he had, had the same feeling. I got goose bumps all over again and so did he.

By now it was dusk and the sun was casting incredible colors over our head onto the desert valley below. There was silver on the sage, while early starlight shown in the east. Golden colored aspen trees along the Rio Grand leave's flickered in the wind below as a assure blue settled into the gullies when a eerie mist rose. Within a few moments all this was gone, to be replaced by a somber pink and then a cool gray. Night was falling. Because we were on the top of the mesa, the shadows were not as long as those on the desert floor. The trees were only lightly covered in shadows, but the spaces in between were still light. The golden light of the sunset shimmered in the wind and as we made way toward the spring it turned to pink, then blue and then blue-gray. Night was about upon us. Presently we came upon a curl of smoke on the horizon, which we thought for sure would be our

Trek guide, waiting for us around a roaring campfire as it gets pretty
cold very fast at those altitudes. As we walked toward the campfire
light we passed a few old bones, a dry buffalo skull and some broken
elk antlers. The wind picked up and began to hiss though the trees
as a storm was approaching. The trees swayed back and forth in an
asymmetric manner so that the their shadows merged into a undulating
mass of dark shapes.

In 30 more minuets we found ourselves with in eyeshot of the
campsite. It was nicely laid out by some willow bushes around the
spring. We could see the light of the fire dancing through the branches
and skipping across the water of the spring. To our relief this was
the camp, already set up, as agreed. A large pot of coffee could be
smelled as we approached from down wind. There was a big pot of
mulligan stew bubbling on the coals and Sam detected the aroma of
fresh corn bread. Sam was the first to pick up the stride and the first
into camp. The rest of us followed in close order no more than five
minuets later. There was a shadow of a man setting just at the edge
of the light projecting from the campfire. Sam hesitated a moment as
Lone Wolf stood up slowly to greet him. Lone Wolf was one of the
few remaining full blood Arapaho Indians left in the area. His family
remained when much of his tribe was moved north to the government
reservations many years ago. They had run away into the hills to evade
being captured. It was a hard life on this dry land but they managed
to survive. But remain he did, and ultimately he opened the Trek and
canoe service.

A heavy chill settled over the campsite as the wind began to pick
up. We could see dances of lightening in the distant clouds as the
spring storms made their way across the desert valley toward us. Jim
reached for several sticks of wood to throw them on the fire to make
it bigger, when Lone Wolf stopped him. Jim was a bit perplexed, and
I guess Lone Wolf understood his question on his face even before
it was asked. He stooped over and handed Jim a tin cup filled with
hot black coffee as they both sat down. Lone Wolf spoke gently as he
asked, "how come you round eyes always build such a big fire? Then
you hot on one side, and cold on the other. Then you must go get
more wood. When Indian build fire, it small one so he can get close

and be warm all over." Jim smiled in sheepish embarrassment nestling his hands around the warm cup to ward off the chill of the cold wind and scooted up closer to the fire.

After we had settled our gear in to the tents, Lone Wolf banged on the bottom of a tin cup with a spoon to call us to dinner. There were no laggards to this call. All of us were hungry and could barely contain our desire to get at that great smelling stew. Lone Wolf dipped his ladle into the bubbling brew and pored out a small portion on the ground as a votive offering (to our surprise). He then began to fill each or our plates. This stew was incredible. There were great chunks of potatoes, whole carrots, corn, squash, and enormous chunks of meat. The broth was not fluid, but almost a thick paste as is befitting a stew that has been allowed to simmer all day. The smell of sage and pepper permeated the air. We all eagerly scooped the hot stew into our mouths. The taste was absolutely wonderful. Salandera, sage, pepper, and well another taste that I could not recognize. But brother was it good. "I asked Lone Wolf what that taste was that I could not recognize." He smiled and said, "round eyes, has never taste buffalo." I certainly had not, so this was a wonderful surprise. The meat was course and ruddy. It certainly tasted good. But I wondered to myself where the dickens he would get buffalo. It was legal for an Indian to kill one that is if they were to be found and most of them were far north of here and or on private ranches.

As the night wore on we all sat contented in front of the fire. The smoke smelled lightly of cedar from the wood we were burning and the coffee was really good. Thank goodness we were out of green goop. It was wonderful just listening to the sounds of the wind, and the occasional chirping of the whippoorwill. From time to time a lone coyote could be heard in the distance, calling out for a mate. After a while we heard a second coyote further out. Over the next one and a half an hour we listened as they sounded each other, getting closer together with each call. Shortly they met with a yelp and the calling was over. I smiled at Lone Wolf who grinned back. He knew that this was the way of things. Soon the wind began to increase in speed. It moaned through the trees again. With it came a threatening brilliant stroke lightening, which flashed in the distance.

Shortly thunder made us shudder as the smell of rain greeted us on the shifting wind.

After a time Jim mentioned the old codger we met at Terlingwa and retold the story that had been told to us. He was certain that it was a hoax and asked Lone Wolf if he knew of such a legend. He said, yes that he had. He knew of the great sadness that had taken place at this very spring, and how the four braves were slaughtered by the buffalo hunters. He knew of Walks-far-woman and her son and how they had been spared by the white man. He knew of the greed of the buffalo hunters and the great wound upon the land that they made off with their lives. He told them of the Indian name for this place, the spring of many sorrows. He knew and lamented the foolishness of the round eyes that would take more than he could eat, who would burn without need of warmth and who would savagely kill a brother for a few animal skins. He said solemnly, "how great the pain of mother earth is to bear such things, there can be no peace until mother earth is healed." Then he began to sing a lamentable song in his native tong, which he would not translate, that raised tremors of fear in all of us. He repeated the same chant over and over again, each time becoming lower and more quieter until it blended with the wind. As the night drew to a close he slipped away into the night (to his tent we thought) and we went to ours.

The following morning we were awakened by the sun as it came across the edge of the tree line surrounding the spring. The combination of warm and cold awoke me. The cool of the dew was all around. It glistened like a million dew diamonds on the grass. It was cool enough to condense your breath as you exhaled. I stumbled half asleep toward the still smoldering campfire. Using my hollow aluminum tent pole I attempted to blow the embers into flames, but to no avail. It was then that I noticed that Lone Wolf's tent was gone. In fact so was the pot of stew, the coffeepot and his blanket. It was as though he had never been there. I could not find where he had struck his tent. There were no holes in the ground from tent pegs. The grass had not been matted down by his tent nor his blanket. There were no footprints leading out of camp. It was very perplexing. What had happened to Lone Wolf.

I woke the others with my discovery, and they too could not find any trace of Lone Wolf either. He was gone, simply not there. It was spooky, we all knew that he was there and the stew we all ate was great. But where was he now? The night before was real or was it was really true? We were all confused. Or was is a dream. We all remember the great stew and the hot coffee, well it sure should have been real. We cooked a small breakfast, struck camp and made our way down the trail in silence each wondering what had happened. All the way down the trail hardly anyone said a thing, and this was hard for Mike to do. This could not have been what they thought might have been a mere dream. Nah not that, after a while, we chatted as we walked across the desert. We all came to the agreement that this was part of the show, part of the western experience. About half way down the trail we stopped for a drink of water and a breather. It seemed that the further along we got, the faster we were walking. I guess it was part all the downhill and part the anxiety about what had happened the night before. We were all educated men, college guys, professional and all smart enough not to believe that silly ghost nonsense. But still the silence spoke volumes.

We stopped at about 10:30 for some rest. As we stood there gathering our breath and enjoying the change of scenery. By now we were far enough along the trail back toward the river to see loblolly pine and other long needle softwoods. You could smell the faint aroma of vanilla in the air that meant Jeffery pines were near. Chip monks and 13 lined ground squirrels chattered in the rocks while yellow-bellied sapsuckers chirped in the near by clump of tall grass. It was a stunning afternoon. Ted caught sight of a Kestrel soaring on silk wings on the eddies, as it road effortlessly up the face of the cliff. It turned swiftly and dove at 200 MPH making a perfect strike on a raven, which went limp, fluttering in a death spiral toward the ground in a hale of feathers. The kestrel swung around with an elegant graceful turn of its wing and swooped down on the dying bird, catching it in mid air. The display of aerial mastery left us completely breathless. No words, just a heart pounding exhilaration at the incredible elegance of mother nature at her best.

Almost as an after thought Mike looked down at the foot of Jim and noticed a Nikon 450 camera resting against a rock Jim was standing on. Jim did not even notice the camera and almost kicked it down the hill when he turned to continue the hike. Mike said, "Hey Jim, hand me that camera", which he did without thinking. "A NIKON . . . whoa . . . a Nikon, that is the worlds best camera!" Jim said, "hey why don't you let me have it. You have one already." Mike retorted, "now Jim, we really ought to turn it into the ranger station. More likely than not someone is going to be looking for it", as he gave it back to Jim. Jim, retorted, "yes you are right, maybe there is a reward and if someone does not claim it then it will be yours". Mike said, "no Jim Yours". Jim put the camera in his pack and we all continued down the trail.

After an hour and a half, a quick drink of iodine treated green-black water from a rain hole (all we could get). With blue teeth and all we made it to the Park Ranger's Head Quarters. Jim turned in the camera as the rest of us waited outside. While we waited on Jim I struck up a conversation with a young ranger who was doing paper work at a table on the porch. I mentioned Lone Wolf and asked him about the legend of Indian Springs. He smiled broadly and said," that we certainly must have gotten our stories mixed up, because Lone Wolf was the son of Walks-Far-Woman, the squaw who survived the buffalo men attack." He then directed us around to the opposite side of the station where a memorial plaque had been placed on a stone monument, by the Daughters of the Texas Republic.

We read the plaque with great interest. It related the story almost exactly the way the old codger in Terlingwa had told it. What really got my hackles up was the date of the incident, 1872 and the fact that Lone Wolf was supposed to be a recluse who lived on the mesa all his days and that he had died there in 1933. He never had a packing and camping company. He was never seen in the valley as he loved the Rim and never came down. A cold chill ran up my back. And apparently that of all the other guys. The trip back to college was uneventfully and almost without talking. We rarely talked about that trip after that. But now 25 years later, I can remember the chilling words of

Loan Wolf when he said, that the sprits of the dead brothers could not rest until the wounds of mother earth were healed. And I guess that we all one time or another have done our part in wounding her, but now that I know better I will do my best to bring back life to the earth rather than take it.

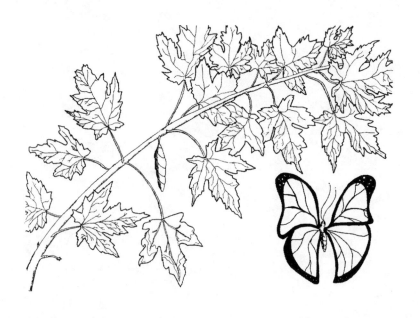

THE CHRYSALIS AND THE KINGDOM

F elix was a monarch, but he didn't know it, at least not at first. It seemed to him that he was a regular person like anyone else and really, there wasn't much different about him. I mean, Felix is such a common name. When he was first born, he looked like so many other babies that lived with him. In fact, his mother could hardly tell the difference between him and all his brothers and sisters. They all looked just alike when they all were crawling around. There was so much activity all the time and things were so confusing that sometimes Felix forgot who he was.

This particular morning it was early spring and the mild summer weather was just around the corner. Those first few weeks of life were so carefree. All there was to do was to crawl around and eat and lay in the warm sun. But mother was always warning the kids to be careful because danger was always around. Felix didn't really believe her until one day, much to his horror, he watched as a gigantic bird carried off one of his sisters. Felix was so terrified that his teeth chattered as he ran for the cover of a crevice in the tree. He had nightmares about that day for weeks afterwards. Mom was right there was great danger for a young caterpillar and from then on he would he more careful. Felix was one of the lucky ones. He managed to survive the numerous bird attacks, which killed nearly half of his brothers and sisters. So for most of the summer he spent eating and growing fat on the rich leaves of the black cherry tree in which he lived.

Felix's mother was always nearby to talk to her children. Though she meant well, Felix thought that she always talked too much. All she would say is, be careful of this, don't do that, watch out for those things, and such. Felix didn't really want to hear all that dumb stuff and most often would simply tune her out. But what really got him was when she used to warn him about climbing to the top of the tree. She would say, there is more to life than just climbing, settle down, son, and then you'll learn how to really live if you will just settle down. "Boy, what a bummer," he would say; "I never get to have any fun; all the other caterpillars are going to the top of the tree, why can't I go." So one day, Felix decided to run away.

Late the next evening, Felix crept out to the edge of the limb that he lived on, then looking carefully behind him to see that no one had followed him and then to the sky to see that there weren't any birds, he jumped onto an adjacent twig and scampered off into the darkness. As he did, he brushed against another caterpillar asleep next to a large knot. Jolted awake, she screamed, "who is it!" It was Ruth, one of his younger sisters. "What are you doing way up here," Felix asked? "Oh, Felix, I got lost and I'm so afraid," she said. "What are you doing out here so high up in the tree? Please help me find Mamma," she said as she started to cry. "Auh, nothing," came his curt reply. "Ruth began to cry harder now as she said, "Oh, I wish Mommy was here. I'm so lonely and afraid. She always told us to be careful and that it was dangerous out here. She told us many times that many many stories have been written and told, and retold about going to the top of the tree." "Ah, shut up, Ruth," Felix said, "you're nothing but a crybaby." "Now look over there," he said, pointing behind him. "All you got to do is to jump over that twig and you'll be home, so go and leave me alone!" "On, thank you, Felix. Let's go," Ruth said. "Nah I'm going this way," Felix retorted. "But Felix, you know what Mamma said about climbing to the top of the tree! You shouldn't do it" Ruth exclaimed. "Ah, shut up, I'm going and that's all there is to it," he said. "Felix, don't go," Ruth said as he wiggled away into the darkness.

As Felix made his way toward the top of the tree, he began to feel new excitement. Wow, he thought, my first adventure. After a while he heard the sounds of other caterpillars crawling around him and he knew he was doing the right thing. The first one he met was a guy named Ralph. "Hey, man, my name is Ralph. Like man, let's go man, we'll be left behind." "Yeah," Felix replied. "Hey, man," Ralph said, "what are you?" "Uh, oh, I'm a monarch. What are you" Felix said? "Yeah, man, that's cool. I'm a gypsy moth, man, a free and wild gypsy moth, man," Ralph responded. After they had crawled a few minutes together, Felix asked where they were going. "To the top, man, don't you know anything? That's where it's at, like everyone wants to be at the top. Hurry up, we will be late," Ralph said mockingly. By this time there were several dozen other caterpillars of different shapes and colors climbing up around them.

It was all so exciting, then whoosh, something fell past them with a faint scream. "What was that," Felix asked. "Hey, man, that was a dude who couldn't make it, man. They just weren't strong enough. They will have to start from the beginning again," Ralph informed him. Whoosh! Another fell past them as they continued to climb. After a couple of hours, they were completely surrounded by hundreds of caterpillars. Everyone was in a hurry pushing and shoving to get ahead. Felix began to become afraid when he saw that he was falling behind Ralph. As he rushed to catch up, he tripped over a caterpillar laying motionless in his path. He must have stopped to get some sleep, Felix thought to himself. Jumping to his feet, he caught up to Ralph and said panting, "boy I thought I lost you." Ralph said, "Come on, runt, we'll be late." By this time, they were very near the top of the tree and the sun was just coming up. It was a beautiful morning and as the sun broke over the horizon, it cast a blue-pink hue over the panorama. Wow, how beautiful, Felix thought. Then looking up ahead, he could see the top of the tree. It seemed to be covered with soft fur shining in the pink light. "Wow," Felix said, "look at that." "Hey, man, yeah," Ralph said, "that's it, that's the top." "Get out of my way it's every one for themselves," he screamed. With that, he kicked Felix in the side of the head and rushed forward. By this time the rush had turned into a stampede as Felix fell, he was walked over by hundreds of stamping feet behind him. Summoning all the energy he had, he struggled to get up and forced his way forward, shoving and pushing, just to stay alive. Soon the rush of caterpillars seemed too large to count. The tide of caterpillars carried him forward. Whoosh, whoosh . . . whoosh, whoosh, whoosh . . . he thought, they couldn't make it. They were too weak. Those turkeys will have to start over from the bottom.

Just as the sun broke over the horizon the top of the tree came into full view. Felix could see the top. Much to his horror, he could see that it was covered with thousands of caterpillars. What had once seemed a beautiful pink fur was in fact a mass of screaming dying bodies all crawling over each other. Everyone was pushing and shoving and kicking and biting. They were climbing over each other, all scrambling to get to the top. And there was nothing there. Felix heard a loud yelp. Hey, that sounds like Ralph he thought. As he looked up, he saw Ralph triumphantly at the top of the tree, screaming wildly waving his arms. Then without warning, a bird swooped down out of the sky and carried him off. Felix was horrified; he was frozen with fear, unable to move. Six other caterpillars stampeded over him in the frenzy to get to the top. By this time, the sun was fully out and the heat had begun to take its toll. Dozens of caterpillars lay dead around Felix and he began to get dizzy himself as he once again struggled to make his feet move. He had gotten only a few inches more toward the top of the tree when the person in front of him slipped and fell, dragging down Felix with him. They both fell to their deaths, unable to reach the top of the tree.

That day was a sad day for all the creatures of the tree. 7,541 caterpillars perished. All of them died in a frenzied rush to the top of the tree and none of them really understood why. Ruth and her mother wept, knowing that Felix's fate was sealed when he ran away. They all wept for his loss. Over time they lost their sorrow in the hurried business of living. Ruth grew fat and full throughout the summer and as summer began to turn into fall, she felt strange urgings come upon her. She didn't quite understand so she asked her mother to explain.

"Ruth," she said, "you must now take your place with all of creation, as I have. I will not be here much longer. I must fly away and you must sleep throughout the winter so you may be born again, renewed and beautiful. I'm sure you can see how different we are. One day you too will have beautiful wings and learn to fly as I have.

But first you must die as your old self. You must learn to love as I have loved, turning from your selfish desires, to love others that they might be fulfilled." "Love," Ruth queried, "what do you mean?" "My child," she said, "love is much like we butterflies. We are beautiful and delicate. Our beauty is to be enjoyed and not controlled. It cannot be compelled. No more than we butterflies can be forced to fly a given strait path. Love is like a butterfly. It is gentle and sweet to look at, yet it is also very delicate. Should you pursue her, she will fly an erratic course, running headlong away from you, for no other reason than that she is being pursued. Even if you should, by chance, catch her and hold her fast, she will die wanting her freedom. Or should you overpower her, she will be crushed by your heavy hand. Yet if you sit still, silently waiting, she will gently flutter to your hand where you may enjoy her beauty for a time. When she does so, do not move too quickly less she flutter away, frightened perhaps never to return again. Therefore rest sweetly in calm repose and wait till she comes to you. When she has arrived, move cautiously, slowly and enjoy her beauty, drinking in all of its richness. But always know that she is never yours to own, less your treasure be crushed by your oppressive spirit. Let her be free. Only then will she choose to come to you to remain there."

"My sweet child, do not do as your brother has done. Do not run headlong for the top, unknowingly. This will only lead to destruction. If you are not crushed by the maddening stampede of the blind, you will surely perish in the competition of so many for one goal. Felix was caught up in the excitement of the chase and he forgot to love. So was pushed along in a mad dash to his death, pursing something that he did not understand nor he could see. He was sustained by his peers who in sympathetic insanity encouraged him to run wildly to his death. Ruth, you must choose the path of life. Stay here, my child, sleep a long winter safe in your chrysalis. Meditate on what I have told you and you shall know the joy of loving as I have. I must go now, my child. Remember to tell the stories I have told you so that our lore will return to educate the young again. It is my time to return to the Creator and rest in His Kingdom, just as it is your time to begin the cycle again," she said. She then started to slowly flap her wings. Ruth lay her head down gently on a leaf as she watched her mother flutter effortlessly over the top of the tree. How magnificent, Ruth thought, what, a beautiful creation a butterfly is, so richly colored. I hope to become all that she was to me, but first I must sleep and when I wake I will understand better how to live in HIS kingdom.

MOHAMMED AND
HIS SHADOW

As Mohammed stood on the top of the lonely dry mesa overlooking the dusty valley below he could see the gently swaying cypress trees and the small specks of people far below him. This rather unremarkable site was all that he knew and all that he loved. His was only a small plot of land next to the town of Al Karj, near the city of Hebron, which his father had inherited from his father whom had willed it to him from his father's father. Many generations had toiled on this small dusty plot of land to provide a meager living for the Jamil family. A few bushels of grain each year and a few goats were all that the land would produce. Now it was Mohammed's turn to take the earth in his hands and to coax a living from the thin, rocky soil. The sun would be unrelenting as it had been for all his clan for many many years. The sun, the toil and the sweat was all that the Jamil family had ever known. Now Fatima, Mohammed's wife was pregnant with their third child, Mohammed knew, he would have to work harder to bring the fruit of the land to his table. But there was a grave cloud upon the land. One, which might destroy all that the clan, had worked for. It was the cloud of despair.

This day was filled with bitterness and hatred. This was a dark day upon the land and the clan. But it had not always been this way. There was a time when the land flowed with green giving water and the people in the valley were filled with goodness and life. But no longer! The darkness of war had descended upon the land and all that remained were the smoking ruins where the village of Al Karj had once stood. No more do the donkey's brae in the early morning. The rooster no longer cries out to protest the rising sun, nor do the doves coo to greet the coolness of the evening. All was laid waist in the aftermath of that dark cloud which came upon the land destroying the village and laying waste to the fields. All there is now are weeping old women and children who have forgotten how to laugh. Only dark patches remain where the wheat once grew. Splintered trees stand in silent testament to the destruction, bowing low, weeping dark ashen tears into the soil. Only sorrow inhabits the valley, only sorrow and desolation remain.

This day Solomon also stands upon the shore of the land he loves. He watches as the waves crash against the stones of the jetty. It is all that remains of what once was a thriving fishing village. The town is gone now; only burned shells of once proud buildings remain. The seagulls no long linger over the fishnets. They have fled and the nets are torn. The beautiful boats of the fishing fleet which once so proudly plowed the foam of the sea now rest on her bottom. Only one small almost inconsequential dingy remains of the 14 wonderful fishing boats once birthed here. He looks upon the desolation and thinks of his wife Delilah, whom is heavy with their second child. He wonders how it could have come to this, . . . only desolation. The gift of the sea, its boats, its catch are little more than a faint shadow of a memory. The Golden Star, which had fed his father and his father's family before him is smashed at the bottom of the harbor. He weeps; wondering what he will do now. Only sorrow remains not even the constant wind from the sea can dry his tears. Only great sorrow remains as their desolate tears fall on the charred ground of what had once been their fishing village.

It was not so long ago that Mohammed and Samson first met. They were young and eager to learn. They were first introduced in Analytical Geometry course where Mohammed as the student teacher and Samson, well not the best of students. But together they managed to get Samson through the torture of mathematics (as he saw it.)

Mohammed was infatuated with the Pan flute that Samson played under the great Juniper Tree in the quad each day after classes. The light, almost flighty melodies he played reminded of his ancestral home and of the hills of Ramalla. Whenever Samson would play Mohammed could imagine the impala leaping from hill to brook through the valleys near his home. He could almost see the rutting young bucks as they leapt on fleet feet from hill to valley and back again when they pranced to attract a mate. His heart soared with the melody, which seemed to free him from the chaos of the city in which he now lived.

Both were students at the American University in Cairo. Both were far from home in an enormous dusty city that was so alien to them. This was as you might except a bit disconcerting for two small town boys. Mohammed was studying applied mathematics and Samson oceanographic sciences. Both were fortunate to receive scholarships, because neither could have ever afforded the cost of airfare much less tuition, books and fees. To each this was a great opportunity to learn of the sciences, of the world beyond their villages and of life itself.

The tumult in Cairo was disconcerting to them. The teaming crush of people everywhere was only broken by the university walls, which offered a small respite from the frenzy of activity outside. Over the months, a friendship grew where once there had been only suspicion. Mohammed loved mathematics and enjoyed the probing questions that Samson would ask. In turn Samson loved the pan flute. They spent many hours sharing each other's gift and giving theirs to the other. This was remarked on the campus that they were a strange pair. Each from such different places, each of a different culture and different faiths. Over time it became as though one was the shadow of the other.

Wherever you would see Mohammed you could also expect to see Samson. Yet despite the taunts and some times threats of their less tolerant classmates the friendship endured and grew. Samson would speak of the sea and his village with lofty words that floated upon the wind and rose into the clouds. Mohammed would weave a magnificent tapestry of words about his home and his land. Both waxed poetically about the great gift of their villages, their land and their sea. Both enjoyed the memory of their homes and they enjoyed sharing it with each other. Both promised, that when they finished school they would each would one day visit the others homeland.

The years of college sped by with such rapidity that neither nearly realized that graduation day had so soon come upon them. Both had to work odd jobs in order to make spending money, and to buy meals. So there was little time for the luxury of parties or disco's. For a time school seemed to settle into a monotonous rhythm of work, classes, study and then more work. In no time at all the years had flown by and with each year they grew more and more brothers at heart.

One spring day after a long day at work they were both relaxing in the courtyard near the great juniper tree with two fellow students when the conversation turned inadvertently to God. After a few pregnant moments of silence they both grinned broadly, knowing that this is a matter better left for another time. They excused themselves from the conversation and walked back toward the dorms. As they walked neither could but wonder what the other might have said. After a time Mohammed said, "Solomon my friend, I know that we are the best of friends and that we are more alike than we are different. But this one issue could destroy our friendship. I propose that we vow never to allow such a thing to happen." Solomon agreed and then he said, "my great friend, you are truly wise to suggest such a thing. I would, however, make one more suggestion." "What would that be?" Mohammed asked? Samson said, "I know that you and I are both great lovers of God, and that we both have great faith in His Goodness, so I suggest that we, each in our own way pray to our God, a daily prayer of protection for the other!" Mohammed smiled broadly nodding his head yes. It was agreed! He started that very week and offered prayers at the Friday Jumah prayer service. Mohammed offered fervent prayer for his good friend Samson, to Allah that he may walk in goodness and safety all the days of his life. Samson for his part prayed daily that sunlight would always fall upon Mohammed's path and that when darkness came into his life that Jehovah would draw him to the protection of the shadow of his wing. With this pact, their friendship grew even deeper. Over the next few months they were seen working and playing the pan flute together, shadow upon shadow. Even those who had taunted them felt a strange peace around them when they were together. It seemed as though their friendship had a life unto itself. Even one of the professors was heard to refer to them as brothers, as though they had come into the world from the same womb.

When graduation day came, Fatima arrived at the train station to meet her beloved Mohammed. Not but two cars behind her was Delilah. When Samson saw her broadly smiling face through the window of the Pullman he rushed right past Mohammed, not even seeing him. Mohammed, for his part was consumed with looking for Fatima. When they met, it was as though all those many years apart had melted instantly into the joy of the moment. He crushed her slim body against himself as though they were to never be separated again. Samson reached up to the window on the train car and gently touched the weeping face of Delilah. Her joy could not be contained as they met at the door. She leapt into his arms in a flurry of joy. He hugged her and spun around and around in delirious delight.

They all went immediately to the graduation ceremony where they were seated on opposite sides of the stadium as they were in different academic departments of the university. When the dean of Mathematics called out Mohammed's name Samson's heart leapt with joy as it swelled with great pride for his good friend's success. Some fifteen minutes later when Samson was called to the podium to receive his diploma Mohammed stood up on the chair, amongst his peers so that he could see better. Great tears of joy welled up in his eyes as he too rejoiced in the success of his great friend. The next few days were a flurry of activity as both packed their belongings, returned their books and put away their small treasures into cardboard box suitcases for the long trip home. Mohammed made haste to pack and taking Fatima he rushed across the campus to Samson's dorm, so that they might meet. Much to his disappointment they were not there because Samson had taken Delilah via a different rout to the dorm of Mohammed. Both were saddened by this odd quirk of fait and as they returned to gather their things to depart for the train station they offered a silent prayer of the others safety.

Then Came the WAR

The devastation that we have spoken of was caused by a Great War. Short-sited politicians started this war like many many others over an inexplicably inconsequential bit of high ground. The war raged little more than a week, yet it consumed two entire armies, killing more than 25,000 soldiers and burning billions of dollars of equipment. Sadly, in this war as in most it is the civilian population who bears the brunt of the destruction. Despite the vastness of the desert where many of the campaigns were fought they tended to focus on the villages where people congregated around water. The sweeping tank battles, which covered hundreds of thousands of square kilometers of life less desert and the wild air engagements, which consumed millions of cubic meters of air, mattered little to the town's people. It is the people who were caught between the clashing titans.

Mohammed was called to active duty from reserve status prior to the shooting war starting as his leaders pondered a quick attack and an aggressive victory over the forces of Solomon's army. His regiment was an anti aircraft unit. They were assigned the unenviable task of protecting the military tarmac at Damascus' main airport. He and his crew of four manned a quad 50-mm radar assisted anti aircraft gun. To their left and right were arrayed in a wide arc 14 SAM missiles and eleven other quads. They felt secure in their protective ring, knowing beyond doubt that they could fend off any attacking aircraft whom might attempt to incapacitate the runway. That night he went to sleep offering a prayer for his family and for the safety of his friend, who was now his sworn enemy in battle?

On the first morning of the war Mohammed was in his bunker when the air raid alarm screamed him to his post. He switched on his radar to find a long random line of blips moving toward him at incredible speeds in excess of 2,400 kilometers an hour. This was unbelievable, had the enemy developed a new fighter or a bomber with such speed. This would be impossible to defeat he thought to himself. But he tried. He scanned the screen for the closest target, set the auto find command and began firing. But to no avail, the speed of these demons was too much. In short succession the first in a line of taxing MIG 29's exploded in a hale of fire and chards of metal. Then the second and then the third. They were blowing up as they taxied out of their bunkers toward the airfield. The fourth aircraft in the line was the Pan Am 747 flight to Tunis. Mohammed closed his eyes, expecting the worst, but miraculously nothing happened. Then the fifth aircraft another MIG exploded showering the hanger with debris. Then the 6th and 7th exploded. The 8th an Egyptian Air 707 was missed. Then the ninth exploded, flipping over a near by Cessna 150 (as thought it was a toy) crushing it. By then the pilots, having witnessed the carnage ahead of them and being blocked in by burning wreckage began to eject out of their taxing fighters. The 10th exploded just as the pilot ejected the canopy. Then the 11th and on and on. In the course of 15 minutes 28 MIG fighters and six Foxbat fighter-bombers were reduced to acrid smoldering twisted metal. Who would have thought that the once proud Darrius Air Brigade would be wiped out so quickly, and without ever getting into the air? The hale of bullets that Mohammed was firing were wasted as his weapon could not track an arc fast enough to catch the demons and there was no manual override to allow him to judge the lead for himself. When the explosions stopped he turned his face away from the smoking ruins and wept. Nothing he had done helped. The SAM missiles fired by his comrades flew widely off target in erratic paths exploding uselessly in the air or impacting in the suburbs. Nothing that they did had any effect upon the attack of the enemy. Nothing worked; it was a complete disaster.

Later that week Mohammed was transferred to long-range field artillery. And for the remainder of the war he was charged with shelling unseen floes thirty or forty miles away. He regularly moved to avoid air attack. It was a dangerous, hard life, but without the constant moving their gun would be destroyed. He moved so many times that he could barely remember where he was much less the targets that they were ordered to attack. He did however remember several engagements in which he was told that he was instrumental in destroying enemy troop concentrations along the coast. This gave him some solace as it was hard to forget the disaster at Damascus.

It was not until almost a year later that he found out what had caused the disaster that day. These blips which moved so quickly were not airplanes at all, they were air to ground missiles fired by aircraft 80 miles away. The AA gun was never designed to kill such a thing and it was no wonder that whatever he did was futile. His enemy had used a Nimrod flying battlefield command and control aircraft to orchestrate the attack from the Mediterranean Sea. Nothing could be done, as his army was unprepared for such a tactic. Although the knowledge that he could have done nothing effective helped him to understand the disaster it did little to swage the shame he felt from having failed in his mission.

That same day Mohammed was called to active duty so was Solomon. Solomon was a fighter pilot in his nations' air force. He felt the indignation of having been subjected to a surprise attack, and he knew the justness of his cause as it was unprovoked and broke countless treaties between his nation and that of Mohammed's. He rose in anger that day to run wildly toward his fighter as incoming attacking aircraft had been spotted only a few kilometers away. His flight chief was already at his F18 when he sprinted up to the bunker. His crew performed flawlessly as they readied the aircraft and armed his missiles and bombs. He quickly mounted the ladder and leapt into the cockpit. The air raid alarm went from attack immanent to attack in process as he launched onto the tarmac. In a few short minutes he was air bound demanding a hard turn on a left departure from the air traffic control zone. Not 500 meters in front of him and behind him were his wingman and teammates. The entire squadron of 25 was air born in little more than 5 minutes. As the last bird made it into the air bombs began exploding on the runway, gouging enormous 75 foot diameter wounds into the pavement. The local air defense commander launched a hale of rockets and bullets, which brought down 8 of the attacking aircraft. As the King David's Belgrade formed cells over the airfield the dogfights began. In a wild melee of wide turns and incredible g's each pilot, friend and foe fought for position to make the kill. The MIG's were no match for the F18's who over the course of the next 5 minutes brought down 11 more aircraft in close order combat. The remaining 5 scattered to the winds flying widely at all elevations to avoid destruction. Solomon locked onto one fleeing adversary whom had swung wide to the north and heading back to Damascus at tree top level. Solomon fired his last sidewinder missile after closing to 1000 meters. The opposing pilot rolled dangerously to the left, clipping the topmost branches of a palm tree, then at the last second executed a air-breaking maneuver and pitched to the right. The sidewinder sped past him just under his left wing. But the proximity fuse exploded the missile in front of his wing. The shrapnel tore holes in it and in the lower fuselage. This slowed him to nearly a stall. The pilot quickly gunned his engine to regain the lost altitude, then trailing smoke and flares continued to make for home. Samson knew that he had only one pass to make the kill before he would loose his quarry in the ridges of the Bakah valley. He carefully lined up his machine guns for the attack. After a few moments he had lock on. He squeezed his finger on the trigger and with three short burst sent his enemy's aircraft exploding into the trees below. Samson yanked back on the stick as the shudder of his exploding foe shook his aircraft. He pushed the throttle back and screamed to 22000 meters in less than a minute, rolling wildly the victory roll as he rose.

A quick check of his radar screen showed that there were no more bogies to be pursued and that all of the attackers had been downed. Orders came over the radio to fly to the nearest target of opportunity and destroy it. He looked down at his fuel gauge to see that he had over a half an hour of fuel yet. As he looked over his right shoulder he noticed a long thin line of trucks making its way down a mountain road trough a village in the valley. This was clearly a troop convoy as he could see five T72 tanks on tank haulers. Without hesitation he swooped down on the unsuspecting convoy. His first pass set the lead truck ablaze blocking the road. Buy the time he turned his aircraft the convoy had backed up into the village, almost bumper to bumper. He leveled his plane, swung low for a strafing run. The first burst sent troops scattering in panic for the fields as they baled out of their vehicles. Only the tanks returned fire. His 20-mm cannon quickly turned 4 of them into flaming hulks. But he overshot the fifth one hitting a fuel truck behind it. It exploded in a furious ball of flames, which set the entire village ablaze. As nothing more could be seen through the flames and smoke he turned toward Damascus knowing that the airport was a prime target and only a few moments away. In three minutes he was on the outskirts of Damascus being bounced by anti aircraft cannon fire. His automatic electronic counter warfare system sent three SAM's scurrying after faux images as he lined up to strafe the hangers and bunkers, which lined the runway. His first pass caused panic on the ground. He skip bombed a 50-KG bomb, which exploded on impact in the fuel farm. It set off a chain reaction. An enormous red and black billowing plume rose to 3000 meters in a few moments consuming all their reserve fuel. He banked to the right for an additional pass as he was buffeted by AA fire. But first he must pass the ring of SAM's and AA guns that protected the fighter bunkers and repair hangers. He dove low at ground level to make his approach. Within a few moments he was lined up on the first AA gun. He squeezed his trigger for the kill, and nothing happened. He squeezed again still nothing. A great lump came to his throat as his heart raced wildly.

Mohammed had seen the roaring ball of flames rise from the fuel farm to his north and had watched the slowly arcing aircraft swing around for his attack on their position. He double cocked his gun, ready to wreck vengeance on the infidel who would dare to attack such a proud air force with such audacity. As the attacking aircraft swung into his line of fire he squeezed his trigger, but only 2 or three shots fired . . . . The gun had jammed; he was at the mercy of the attacker. Mohammed trembled as sweat broke upon his brow. All he could do was to watch as death bore down at him from the air at 1200 km per hour. There was no time to run for the bunker and the only thing he cold do is close his eyes and pray the death prayer. As the jet flew over the jet wash blasted his helmet off, sprayed him with sand but did not fire. This was incredible, surely he had me in his sights and he did not shoot. En-sh-Allah, Mohammed thought it is the will of God that I not die this day. A great rush of relief came across him as he relaxed. He turned to watch the aircraft bouncing through AA fire disappear into the horizon as quickly as it had arrived.

Investigations later showed that the gun had been jammed by a warped shell so that it could not be fired. Apparently one bullet was bent enough to cause it not to be thrown out by the extractor. The blame for the failure of the gun was not placed on Mohammed, whom initially had been accused of failure to perform his duty. This was as one might guess a great relief to him, as the firing squad was the reward for such inaction. But it would be more than a year before he was to find out the results of the inquiry. This was as you might guess a very difficult year. He spent many sleepless nights wondering if he would ever see his beloved Fatima again. His anger grew and his pain was immense.

Solomon flew back to his base, shot up by the AA fire and near by explosions of arrant SAM's. But he did not think that he had suffered any serious damage, even though the stick was sluggish. No warning lights were activated. He arrived nearly out of fuel. It was quickly apparent from the damage on the airfield that the main runway was unusable. Although the civil engineers were working rapidly to repair the damage, they were slowed by the thousands of bomblets, which had to be cleared by the explosive ordinance disposal team. He looked at his fuel gauge and declared a fuel emergency. The tower immediately vectored him the secondary emergency landing field some 25-km away. He retorted that he was flying on fumes and could not make the alternate field. He was given immediate landing instructions to land on the parallel taxiway where an emergency aircraft-arresting barrier had been erected. He turned for the taxiway, which looked inexorably small, compared to the primary runway. And that it was, since he was used to landing on 50-meter wide runways the 15-meter taxiway looked like a thin black line. As he lined up his approach his fuel warning light came on, . . . out of gas. The engine sputtered, then coughed and then flamed out. It was going to be a dead stick landing at 250 km per hour and only one try, no way to come around again. He pulled back on the stick to flare, fixed his ailerons and adjusted the trim tab. One might have hoped that this aircraft would glide further but fighters quickly turn into dead rocks when the power is gone. He dropped precipitously fast as he banked for the final approach. The stick was very heavy, as the hydraulic system no longer had power to run the compressors. It was rapidly becoming apparent he was not going to make the end of the approach zone. He had to make a quick decision, to punch out now and loose a $58,000,000 aircraft that was badly needed for the defense of the nation, or to attempt to make the impossible landing. Then it occurred to him that he had one small bit of energy left in this bird. He reached down, removed the switch cover from the firing button and punched the emergency starter. Although there was no fuel to restart the engine the resulting explosion of the hydrazine might just give him enough forward momentum to make the landing. As the hydrazine exploded he experienced a rush of 2.8 g's, which almost caused him to black out as he banged his head against the seat rest. But it was enough to get him to the firm pavement. He landed with a loud bang as he flared at the last minute. But now he was rolling to fast for the bumpy taxiway. The sympathetic vibrations would cause his landing gear to collapse if he did not slow down. He applied his wheel brakes, then his air brakes. The aircraft began to slow, for a moment. Then the air brakes locked at 15 degrees up angle, not enough to be effective. Apparently the AA did more damage than he thought and the bang was the sound of the hinges freezing. Riding the brakes hard he slammed into the arresting barrier which whirred loudly as the catch real spun out the cable in a plume of blue green smoke. When the drum reached the end of the tape it snapped and the jets front landing gear collapsed. The noise of the jet slammed into the pavement in a hail of sparks and then slid off into the soft sand, coming to rest some 25 meters into the dirt in a spray of dust. A rush of fire fighting equipment sped down the tarmac and were upon the jet in less than a minute with water spraying. Just as the dust was being settled by the water spray from the fire trucks, Solomon popped the canopy and emerged unharmed. Wide grins were all around and as were wise cracks about how Solomon would have to repay the taxpayers for the damage to the aircraft.

A year later the incident reports would show that the aircraft was easily repaired and ready to be flown in 24 hours. And that Samson's actions were not only very brave but also crucial in saving a critical air force asset desperately needed for the counter attack. It also showed that his gun had jammed on the last chain of bullets, which had somehow gotten 10 degrees askew. This should have normally caused it to ignite as it was an incendiary, but by some miracle it did not and the aircraft was spared an deadly internal fire. By the grace of God Solomon thought I have been kept safe.

It was not long there after when the war ended as all wars do. Samson and Mohammed both returned to their respective homes. They returned to great sorrow and great destruction sponned of the conflict. Mohammed's wife who had given birth to a son in his absence was very bitter. She cursed the enemy for the destruction of their home and the burning of their grain fields. She railed in righteous indignation against the infidels who would attack the defenseless village and kill so many of their clan. She swore an blood oath that her new son would one day wreck the same havoc on their enemies as they had done to them. She could do little more than weep in the arms of Mohammed, who also felt the anger of vengeance swell within him. Also after a time Mohammed chided her lovingly, to not let the pain of today curse the next generation. Together they wept for those who had been lost and prayed for help to rebuild. After a time Mohammed remarked to his wife about the incident in Damascus and how Allah had spared his life that day. He also reminded her that not all of the enemy were bad, as he remembered his lost friend Solomon. They were both grateful. Ultimately they made resolve to offer a daily prayer of thanks for the protection he had received. With time they gathered the broken stones of their home and built another on the same land. Over the next few weeks they gathered the scattered flock, salvaged the farm tools and began to live again.

When Solomon returned to his village he to was met by his wife, she was in tears for the destruction of the fishing fleet and their lively hood. They both stood in the ruins of their house, with their newborn son in her arms they both stood there stunned by the utter blackness of the destruction. In a fit of uncontrollable rage Delilah cursed the enemy's artillery barrages which had destroyed so much. She cursed those who had such an evil heart; she spat upon the ground cursing them to receive exactly what they had given to them. Solomon pulled her close as she coddled her and said, My Love do not do such a thing, less we condemn him to the same pain (as he pointed to his son.) He reminded her of his affection for Mohammed and told her that not all of the enemy were beast. They stood there for a moment and just rocked each other in their love and after a time she understood. They too found the strength to rebuild. They were able to get a government loan with which to buy an new boat. Within eight months they were in their new home and fishing in the new boat the "Rising Star." It seemed that life would once again become good. Samson especially enjoyed having his son Samuel with him as he went to sea. In time Samuel would inherit the boat and become the seventh in a long line of proud fishermen of the village.

It was more than 15 years later and sadly two more wars when the political situation calmed down enough for Samson and Mohammed to both attend a college reunion. My god Samson thought 25 years since I have been to the university. I wonder who I will see. Secretly he feared that Mohammed had perished in the wars. As so it was the same for Mohammed. He longed for his old friend and wondered as well if he had been killed in the wars.

The reunion was to last three days and as chance would have it, the activities from the mathematics and oceanographic departments kept them apart. It was not until the evening of the last day that Mohammed, while walking back to the cafeteria with is wife and son heard the faint melody of a pan flute wafting across the quad. It was undeniably Samson's technique. Mohammed' s heart leapt with anticipation. He rushed ahead of his wife and pushed his way thorough the throng of people milling around in the courtyard. He rounded the corner, and at the spot where he and Samson used to meet, under the great juniper tree. There was a small boy playing the pan flute. Mohammed stopped for a moment, with his heart stuck in his throat and tears welled up in his eyes. Oh my God, he thought, it was not Samson. After a few moments of listening to the memories that the music brought to mind he turned to sadly walk away. As he turned Samson greeted him with a great hug. Both of them jumped together with great affection in a flurry of laughing and simultaneous talk. The tumult caused the boy to stop playing at which point Samson said, "son come here." It was Samuel who had learned the pan flute and its unique technique form his father. After a few moments Mohammed's wife Fatima joined the reunion with a bit of motherly suspicion on her face. Sulayman-al-Ackmed, her 38-month-old son was in tow. They were joined a moment later by Rachel who scooped up Samuel into her arms. They were to be introduced to the family of Mohammed. After some minutes of uncontrollable tear filled joy they agreed to meet that evening at the restaurant for dinner.

Samuel arrived first with his father Solomon. Delilah had a head ache (actually she instinctively felt that this was not a place for her that night) so she did not come. Mohammed arrived a few minutes later with Sulayman, and gave an excuse that Fatima was tired. She too knew that this was a time for the men and she would only get into the way. Solomon set the boy down and hugged Mohammed who offered a kiss to each cheek in return. They began to remissness hardly even noticing the meal or much less that the two boys had wandered off into the courtyard. There were so many years to catch up on. On how the farm was doing, what a good catch they had that year and how they had both managed to survive the wars.

In time the conversation turned to that horrible day in Damascus. Mohammed relayed how Allah had protected him that day and that the aircraft did not fire, and how his AA gun had jammed and how he almost got court-martialed. Samson listened with wide-eyed aghast as he listened to the story that Mohammed told. He then told Mohammed that he too had a similar situation happen to him. Both held their breath a moment daring to believe the impossible. They continued to compare notes and translated the dates between the Arabic and Georgian calendar. To their great shock they discovered that it was Mohammed at the gun and Samson in the aircraft. They both confirmed it by identifying the markings on the airplane and AA gun. They simultaneously realized in horror that day they were shooting at each other. A pregnant moment of heart pounding silence followed when the sound of the pan flute wafted out of the courtyard. Solomon remarked that perhaps Allah and Jehovah had conspired that day to protect them both. Mohammed agreed saying that Allah always hears the prayers of the righteous. Solomon agreed that Jehovah heard such prayers also.

They both rose together to follow the sound of the music. The found both their sons seated near the fountain at the center of the dining room. Samuel teaching Sulayman the pan flute. Both were completely entranced with their activity, not noticing their fathers had come to watch. This moment needed no words. Mohammed and Solomon knew that perhaps one day their son's may be sparred the tragedy that they had lived. As the evening ended they both hugged profusely, pecking each other on the cheek, as was the custom at a farewell. Solomon remarked that perhaps one day their sons would also become such great friends. Mohammed remarked, "En-sh-Allah! Perhaps they too will have a shadow!"

TOMORROW

It was a cold dismal day on earth when Satan surveyed his domain. Many trials had fallen upon mankind, earthquakes, famine, war and pestilence had devastated society. The Devil and his ghouls were having a riotous field day. The slender thread upon which civilization's order had been hung was cut and chaos prevailed. In every part of the world riots and violence were the order of the day. Moscow and New York had been reduced to ashes by war. Paris was a turmoil of murder, fire, death and insurrection. Bogotá and Caracas had been razed by an earthquakes. Race riots had destroyed much of South Africa's large cities. Pretoria's streets ran red with white blood. Peking was heaped high with bodies piled upon bodies in a desperate attempt to regain order. Nowhere on earth was there any peace. All of mankind was cast into a sea of death and reoccurring violence. The very foundations of culture and civilization were about to crumble into ashes. It seemed as though even the elements were at war with man. With them they brought even greater destruction and death.

The clouds held back their rain on the Great Plains of North America and on the Pampas of Argentina. The ensuing drought destroyed virtually every blade of grass and every stalk of grain. The snows fell mercilessly on Northern Europe leaving it paralyzed under ice. The heart of North Russia and deepest part of Africa were besieged by a torrent of unforgiving rains. The floods swept away everything man made in their paths. The whole of Nairobi was washed away in one night when the Nigeria River Dam collapsed washing 820,000 people to their deaths in the sea. Famine spread across Northern Africa as the droughts came, with them came the locust. Crete and Turkey were thrown into ruin by a succession of earthquakes, pyroplastic flows and volcanic ash. The tidal wave caused by the catastrophic explosion of Mt. Vesuvis obliterated Naples, Italy devastated every major port of North African Coast and in Southern Europe. China's billions faced starvation with the coming of repeated natural disasters, one after another. Throughout the world all hope had died. All that remained was death, dying and absolute chaos. The pervading stench of rotting flesh could be smelled everywhere. Illnesses once thought to be extinct ravaged every land; no country was exempted from the curse. Plagues of strange and fearful insects consumed what little foliage was left and when men tried to crush them they stung back with the intense searing pain of a scorpion. Nearly a third of all trees died, when the massive amounts of smoke from countless fires dimmed the sun. Mankind's plight was desperate and there was nearly no hope that he would survive.

Late that evening Lucifer called together a council of his demons in Hell. As they gathered around a large burnt round table among the smoke and sulfur he screamed, "demons and ghouls, fellow Devils I'm proud of you, at last, at long last after more than 12,000 years our time has come. We reign supreme over the earth, torture and death abound. Everywhere there is despair. The destruction at last is nearly complete. We have completely murdered the peace. Now you disgusting ghoul's report to me on the sections of the world in your charge, I want to know the extent of *My Glory*."

Lucifer, pointing to his left as fire jumped from his fingertips said, "Lackey" report to me your beautiful works of destruction. Lackey my favorite, what have you done for me today." "Ah, Boss I done good today. I've been tu' Australia. I instigated a coup in the government . . . . Ha, ha, ha, the Neo-Nazi's Party has taken control of the country. We are on our way to grand chaos, and more war."

"What." . . . Lucifer said. "Is that all you've done, considering the state of the world, is that all, You know the wild successes we have been having and all you could do is to engineer a coup for the Nazis." Lucifer stood up spitting smoke and fire from his nostrils he screamed, "take him away. I'm going to make an example of him.

Throw him into the lake of fire. Let him burn, but torture him first, pull out all of his fingernails and all of his teeth, set his tail on fire. Get him out of my sight. Get him out of here I won't stand for such incompetence." With that three large ugly multi headed beasts took Lackey screaming out of the meeting room and threw him down into the smoking pit.

With a sly toothy smile, Lucifer said, "Now fellow demons what have you to report today. You Aghast, what have you done." Aghast approached the podium sheepishly and says, "Uh . . . , boss I have spread distrust throughout North America. I started the great northwestern forest on fires that have nearly consumed three northwestern states. They have been burning for three and one half weeks now, isn't it wonderful. It sort of reminds me of home you know. Considering the drought I brought on they will easily burn for three weeks more." "Excellent, Aghast, excellent, keep up the good work." Satan said.

"Now you Logorrhea what have you done." "I've been to Europe and Central America. There is a great revival on now because of my work. I've fooled people into thinking that they can appease the calamity with the ancient pagan ritual rites. Many witches, and warlocks abound. I've gotten the druid cult back on its feet in England and Ireland. They are sacrificing babies again. and I am just getting started. Northern Ireland is going well, why there is full-blown civil war going on right now. There were 47 bombings last week alone. Not to mention the riots in Dublin. I got the Celtic rites back on solid ground and everyone all over Europe is turning to adultery and lust. Church attendance is way down and I've gotten most of the cathedrals turned into museums. Any way the ones that haven't been burned down yet. There is civil war in Chile and Ecuador is poised to attack Peru again. I am having a wonderful time, can I go back to do some more, boss, can I, can I, can I?"

"Good, good," Lucifer said, "Now what about you, Apocalypse. What have you done?" "Well, boss, I started a massive flood in Central China. I got them to cut down all the trees in the name of patriotic capitalism. What fools they are. I drowned over 11 million people in three months, isn't it wonderful. And I haven't even started my plagues yet. I have set up Sun worship temples all over Asia. There is a great revival, since the communists came, they have been so helpful." "Ah, Apocalypse you are a ghoul after my own heart. Keep going, tell me more," Satan said. "I've poisoned the Yellow River and the Mekong with industrial pollution. In fact the toxic mix I have concocted will last for centuries. Not one thing will grow and their deltas are sterile this season, not one grain of rice will be eatable. And Cambodia is my greatest triumph. Genocide, wonderful complete genocide AGAIN, I've totally eradicated the Khmer Rouge and 3/4 of the peasant population as well. GOD I love how stupid these people are," Apocalypse said. "Hey watch your language, I won't have profanity used in my presence" Lucifer said. Then he said, "Ah, yes, I've planned that for some time, good, good . . . very gooooood!!!"

He then points to his right. "You, Hypocrite, what have you done?" "Ah, ha, I've been to Africa. There are full-scale wars going on across the continent, and I got em all started. Nigerian genocide was nothing compared to what is about to happen in Rwanda. Since they exploded their first atomic bomb things have gotten lots better. Namibia is becoming a blood bath of intertribal intrigue just like Angola. I've arranged for the wholesale massacre of thousands of sympathizers on both sides. Not even the beasts of the jungle escaped the chemicals that they are using. What a delight to see all those vultures so fat." Lucifer said, "Good, good, Hypocrite, good."

"Now, Esoterica, my sweet, seven headed beast. What have you done for me?" Lucifer said. Esoterica replied with a wide toothy grins, "we, (he says with a hissing sound) Master, have been very very busy. We have clogged the coastal seas with pollution and choked the fish into submission. The air over all major cities of the world is delightfully lethal. And we have planted a time bomb in the earth's soil. We have poisoned it with eutectic salts. Soon no land anywhere will produce any food. They will all be barren, burned beyond use by the salts. Isn't that exciting. We have been to Asia Minor and to India. There we have sown discord and violence and terrorism. The Hindus are killing the Muslims again. And they are both killing the Seks. I have also widened the latest Afghanistan war. Iraq is in ruins. The killing is everywhere. We have confused many that suicide will bring them to heaven. These wars have spilled into Nepal and over the boarder to the north. Isn't it absolutely wonderful. Even the Iranians are getting ready to attack Afghanistan. No one in the region is free of its curse. We have been especially busy in Taiwan and Japan who are strangling under our pressure. We have dulled the minds of their leaders. Their people are crucifying Christians once again, just as like in the good old days. With Japan at war with Taiwan we can expect a great blood bath by the end of the month. There will be a great harvest of lost souls. Soon it will spread to the main land, as it did in the late 1930's and early 1940's. I LOVE IT, I LOVE IT, I LOVE IT!!!! We have succeeded once again with inciting suicide for the Emperor. Oh yes, we almost forgot, Manila, I rocked the Philippines with a 200 mph typhoon and Manila no longer exists. It's rubble, nothing but rubble, all else was blown away, it was completely flattened!!!! . . . did I do good boss????"

"Now you, Profanity, what good curse do you have for me!" Lucifer said. "Master, Master, Apathy, I've got Apathy" he replied . . . . "What!!! is that all you can say," Satan screamed cursing him. "No, no, wait, master, wait . . . it's worldwide. The Jews have turned from the temple and are involved in daily sacrilege. Hardly any Jewish family keeps the Sabbath any more. But that's not my greatest triumph. The Americans, they don't care any more, they don't care about anything. They are complacent in their fatness and I've gotten the God is Dead rumor revived again. Priests and preachers are leaving the ministry by the droves. Nuns are diverting their teachings to social issues. No one cares about God any more. And I've nearly gotten the war clouds gathering over the Middle East. And they don't ever see them. Ha! I expect a nuclear holocaust by the end of the year, what a victory that will be" Profanity responded. "Ah, yes," Lucifer says as smoke fumes out of his nostrils and he drools, "I can hardly wait. I can smell the sweet stench of rotting flesh already."

As he is speaking a small messenger ghoul crawls in on his stomach like a serpent and hands Lucifer a slip of soldering paper. Lucifer reads it, his eyes get large and his grin falls from his face. Standing slowly up he raises his gnarled hand to stop all the chattering. A dead silence falls upon the assemblage . . . . Lucifer, reading the note says, "It says here that Jesus has announced over all radios and TV networks simultaneously in all languages that He is returning in two weeks. It says He called everyone to repent and to come to Him by then or be lost.!"

A great clamor arose out of the meeting room. Esoterica said, "Hey, Master, that's not fair it's not written in the book that way. The Bible says," Satan jumps up and screams "Stop, I don't want you to mention that foul wretched book in here ever. EVER!!!!." "Lackey, what do you think we should do? Aghast, what is your advice, Apocalypse give me a plan, we must have a plan. Hypocrite where are you, Hypocrite where are you when I need you. What do we do? For a few moments confusion proliferates as all the demons talk at once in a grand Chaos . . . . Then Lucifer raises his hand once again and all are silent. "I know, what we will do he says with a slithering smile. We will have them postpone it.", "What," comes the cry from the assemblage. "Yes," Lucifer says, "with a toothy smile, we'll fool the people again, after all they have two weeks, and you can always do it tomorrow. Yes, yes, we will have them put it off", he said with a roaring laugh. With that the meeting is adjourned and the demons and ghouls are dispatched to the four corners of the world to carry out their master's plan.

THE MASTER IN THE FIELD

Imagine that you are on the edge of a large meadow on a bright sunny spring day. It's early spring and you can smell the multitude of flowers in the field. Their succulent smell greets your nostrils on each breeze filling them with great delight. The flowers are scattered like multi colored paint spattered from an artist pallet across a green carpet of grass. You can see the bright green trees radiant in their new growth. The tall ponderosa pines seem to reach up and touch the sky. As you look across this beautiful panorama you can almost taste the pine pollen in the air. The sky is rich blue dotted with cotton clouds. The sun is peeking out from behind a cloud as a shower rays of warmth rain down on the valley. You begin to walk and as you walk you feel the moistness of the dew from the grass on your feet and you know it's good and it's cold. You happen to stumble upon, a small brook gurgling through the grass. You savor the sweetness of its sound and the rich beauty of the clear motion of the water.

The gurgling of the brook is welcomed melody to your ears. You see trout darting from bank to bank and leaping over the wet rocks, seeking the cover of the overhanging grass. Their rich red and soft golden gray color of their sides is pleasing to your eyes. You want to stretch out your hand to touch them. But you know that you cannot. It is so good to be alive you think. What a wonderful and magnificent day that this is! Wouldn't it be something if all the days were like this one, you think to yourself? It is so good to be alive, to feel and to hear and smell and to taste all of this goodness. The sound of the running water is so inviting. It beckons to you to touch it. The sound is refreshing after the hustle and bustle of the day. As you stop and touch that crystal clear water it almost numbs your hand, it's so cold. You look and see the fish swim free and alive darting from rock to rock, skittering along the bottom of the creek stirring up swirls of sand which are slowly washed down stream. You take in a deep breath of fresh clear air and you say "My God, how can I not believe?"

Then, you look up in the clouds and you see a hawk flying free on wingtips from cloud to cloud just as if he were floating free. As each wing tip spreads and folds the bird seems to pulse with the life around him and to sing to God that HE is in all things. As the hawk draws in its wings and pushes them out again, sailing on the wind your heart soars with it. You begin walking gingerly across the brook because you don't want to get wet. Carefully, gingerly you pick your way across the wet stones. Then unexpectedly you slip. Moving quickly to catch yourself, you tumble headlong into the brook. The water is so cold that it takes your breath away. Shocked and gasping for air you quickly stand up ankle deep in ice-cold water. More embarrassed and surprised than hurt you chuckle at the silliness of the moment. The water runs quickly off our clothing as the warmth of the sun and the light breeze begins to blow away the embarrassment. The renewed warmth of the sun is such a welcomed gift. It steals away the chill and brings goodness to your skin. Squishingly you pick your way out of the creek bed and start to walk slowly down the meadow toward the valley.

As you begin to walk down what appears to be a path (it's not much of a path just a few pebbles at first) you take in another deep breath of the refreshing cool air as you walk on. There are only a few bare spots among the pebbles. You look down and you see the beautiful field of flowers again. Except this time you are so much closer that you can distinguish each dot of color as an intricate vibrant blossom. The rich red of the poppies, the vibrant yellow of the sunflowers beyond them and the deep purple of a small flower you can not identify radiate with life. All of the colors seem to vibrate as they sway in the gentle breeze. The Queen Ann's Lace is stark white in union with the multicolored dotted smallness of the other flowers, but it too is gently waving a greeting to you in the breeze. You reach down and you feel the wetness of the dew on them. You can almost taste it with your fingers. Their colors are so intense in the morning sun that you almost expect them to stain you fingers as you touch the flowers. As the breeze shifts you smell them again. The smells are mixed in a delightful profusion. It is incredible as aromas of wild rose, lilac and morning glory wafts across the air and fills your nose. The rich nectar tickles your nose with delight. You can feel, in some small measure the excitement that a butterfly feels as it tastes the multi colored goodness that the flowers offer. The sun dances across them as though they were alive changing their colors into a many hued array only rivaled by the rainbow. Shadows cast a mocking counterbalance to the brilliance of the sun's rays. How wonderful to be here, to be alive to taste the goodness of the valley. It is so good to be alive and to drink in all the goodness that the Master has created here.

As you begin to walk down the valley you notice that the path starts to become more narrow. You look to your left and then to your right. You are enthralled by the grand majesty of the trees. Oh how beautiful they are against the sky, the greenness so much alive. The breeze causes the same interplay of sun and shadow as you saw on the flowers, except it is more subtle. They are cast into gray, light green and dark green forming a rich kaleidoscope of rich life. You enjoy the contrast of the bright green new growth against the darker older pine needles. It is wonderful. As you walk you grasp a branch shaking it. A light yellow green shower of pollen rains down upon you and is carried away by the breeze. The trees seem to be dancing as the wind gently pushes and pulls their branches too and fro. Each branch objectingly resists brother wind then yields with a gentle whooshing. The whole forest sings this subtle, gentle song as the wind dances among the branches and across the grass.

As you walk a bit further you see the clouds have begun to come together and the late morning has passed into noon. How sweet is the experience of the warmth of the sun shining on your body. You remember still the moistness from the creek and you smile all over again at the contrast. You stand there with your eyes closed for a moment absorbing each ray of life. It gives you such warmth, it's so good, so warm so reassuring. Unexpectedly a shadow flashes across your face, you quickly open your eyes to look up! Again as you continue to walk down the valley you drink in the beauty that surrounds you. You can see that the valley has become more narrow now. It seems as if you are being drawn into an opening at the edge of the forest. The clouds have now absorbed most of the sky and you can feel coolness of the breeze as it begins to blow a bit harder. It seems as though the rain is about to come. You can taste it in the wind as its fresh new smell warns you. You can smell it as you walk on under the trees. A few sprinkles of wetness hit your arm and your legs. You instinctively seek the shelter under the arms of the trees.

You wait there a moment then you lean next to the tree to smell the gentle, oh so gentle fragrance of the bark. The pines are so sweet that you can almost taste the texture of their needles. You reach up and play with a bit of the sharpness of a needle as your press you finger against the end. You can smell the rich pinesap as it runs down an adjacent cone. You rub your hand across the coarseness of the cone and catch the sticky substance on you fingertips. Lifting them to your nose you smell the pungent strength of the tree. You muse at the promise of life to come held within the armored cones and you smile. You feel so alive and so free as you walk further. Now the forest now seems to be closing in around you. You look back down the valley, then up ahead again. You are getting concerned. You know it's almost as far back as it is forward (you think to yourself should I or shouldn't I go on). Unreasonable apprehension peers into your mind as you consider if you should go into the forest or return to the valley. After a moment you decide that this is a good day. So you move toward the forest, with caution. Continuing into the forest you can see that the trees now have taken new shapes; they are a bit darker now. As the part of the sun peeks around from the edge of a cloud they appear less friendly. You guess that the trees are getting thicker as they seem to be covering the sky with profusion. You feel a slight uneasiness, which you do not welcome. You think to yourself, "I liked the meadow maybe I'll go back, no well . . . uh . . . it is almost as far back to the meadow as . . ." I'll continue down the path. Almost without noticing it a small fear begins to grow in you. "I don't know what I'm afraid of," you think to yourself. Then you look around and you see that the darkness of the

forest has become overbearing. You look to the left and then to the right and you cry out, "Oh why did I ever come down this trail," . . . Then you notice that your pace has begun to move a bit faster as you want to quickly move through the darkness. You duck under countless trees whose silently cursing branches push against your progress. The once beautiful trees have now taken on plaid green gray and gray black sharp shapes. Their once majestic branches seem to be mere shadow of their once opulent beauty. They extend out a sharp angles without leaves, trusting upward in a vain attempt to reach the sun which will not show itself. Their sharp dead edges of the branches tug at your clothing as you try to pass. The cold pallid moss resists you passing and clings to you like spider webs. The deep earthy smell of the moss is repugnant and unwelcome.

You begin to move faster now. You are stepping over logs, moving faster now. After a short time you stop to catch your breath. You can see that you are completely surrounded by the forest and the sun has been choked completely off by the tall trees. Your heart pounds uncontrollably as you stand there not sure which way to go. Then a tear works it way down your cheek. And you feel so alone, you wonder what it was that drew you into this cold dark lonely place. It's so cold in here so lonely. "My God why did I come here," you think to yourself. I'm so tired and afraid. A cold chill runs down your back as the wind bristles through the pines with an uneven hiss. The cool of the rain has turned into deep cold that bites at your skin and objectingly rifles trough your hair. The chill turns to goose bumps and then the goose bumps turn into fear. Your thoughts race through the shifting shadows when you hear a branch make a loud crack. You imagine a beast is moving in your direction so you begin to run as a flush of adrenaline spins your feet on the dew-moistened grass. Stumbling forward you lurch toward a large stump. Coming to rest with a thump against its outstretched jagged branches tearing at your clothing you leap to your feet, as the wind brings another ominous crack. The imagined beast is getting closer. You leap over the stump and begin to run away form the sound. As you run, the bushes object even more to your passing, pulling against your hair, grabbing against your pants and your shirt. The faster you run the more they object. Soon they are grabbing at your movements with great violence. They refuse your passage as you fly forward blindly away from the unseen evil, which is behind you. The course bark of the trees screams against your hands as you make your way through the gray black shadows. The wind stirs the branches into an eerie dance among the shadows. Each motion creates a new shadow, which mocks your movement through them. The branches flash like beacons across your face as your labored breath is seared by the cold wind. You run faster and faster away from what you cannot see and you can only hear. Faster and faster you run, stumbling over roots that jut out to stop you. Leaping over a fallen tree, which grabs your feet. It pulls you down to the earth with a thump. Looking up, forward, you see a small light. The taste of the moist earth is harsh in your mouth. Spitting it out you regain your feet and start to run again. Sweat is pouring down your face, mocking your movements in salty exhalation. You move forward, slower now, as fatigue begins to drag upon your limbs. You struggle with all your might but your tired limbs can only pull you slowly away from the darkness behind you.

Turning back and forth, searching with every iota of energy in your mind you look for the unseen beast you know is fast upon your heals. You toss your head left then right then left again hoping to catch a glimpse of the unseen danger. As you see again a light at the end of the path you notice that it has become even brighter. It is strangely warm and it seems to pulsate. You want to move toward it, but you do not know why. It pulses with an erratic array of beams that dance objectingly through the underbrush. With each pulse it draws you closer to it. Almost magnetically it draws you to it. "What could this be." you ask yourself? Without knowing why you begin to move in its direction. The warmth of the glow mesmerizes you. Its radiance is so strikingly different than the cold of the afternoon around you, you cannot resist it. You push your way through the underbrush, which still pulls you back, tearing at what remains of your shirt. Soon you can see it much better now as you are getting closer. The light is a deep gold umber color. It seems to radiate from a center point. It pulsates with a harmonic rhythm that flickers between the branches of the trees. It is calling to you. It seems to be calling out your name, it wants you to come toward it. It even seems to be moving slowly toward you as your move toward it. The light seems to be alive. You can barley see the light through your sweat clouded eyes. But you can see that it is moving. You are sure now that it is moving . . . . It seems to brings warmth, which you can feel contrasted on your face as the wind from behind brings a wet chill to your body. You look squinting past the cloudiness in your eyes. And because of the brightness you are not sure which way it is moving. So you stop a moment to wipe your eyes and you can see that it is true, what you had hoped for is true, it is moving toward you. You can hardly believe it as you gasp for air in your tiredness. It seems to have a shape. The shape is taller than it is wide. It seems to flow out of the light, from the light, and is the light all at the same time. You instinctively slow your pace, in caution and shade your eyes with your hand from its increasing intensity. The light beckons you forward. It pulsates its welcoming call to you. You open your eyes just a bit to see what is this thing that is in the light. It has a shape that is familiar, but you cannot quiet make it out. "What is it, you think to yourself, what is that shape? Does it look like . . . . ?" Then with a flash of insight you can see it does have a shape. You recognize it in a split second of understanding. It is a very common shape. It is a shape well known to us. It has the shape of a man . . . . Unbelieving for a moment you hesitate. You squint again bringing your eyes to bare tightly on the shape. Yes it does have the shape of a man. You pause perplexed wondering what manner of illusion this is. Could this be a mirage? Could this be merely an imagined portion of a dream? Is this only a long lost desire born of exhaustion? You think, "am I loosing my sanity . . . have I driven my body too fast too far and caused my mind to falter?"

As you again begin to move toward it again you can see that yes it has the man. Yes indeed it is a man! And he appears to be covered by a robe, which is fluttering ever so slightly in the breeze. He seems strangely familiar but you cannot as yet make out his face. His radiant glow draws you to him . . . It's so warm, so inviting, so peaceful. You don't seem to be able to stop yourself as you begin to walk faster toward the figure. You can see clearly now that this is indeed the figure of a man. He is standing looking at you with his hands crossed in front of his lap. He waits for you to move forward as the radiant light around him bathes all the trees in a golden hue. You move closer to Him now. You glance to your left and right where you can see that you have moved into a small golden meadow. Gazing back a the figure, you know in your heart that this man is familiar. He seems like a long lost friend whom you have nearly forgotten. The sight of him brings you satisfaction, which you cannot understand. You continue down the path, which has become wider now. You push yourself forward trying desperately to see who this might be, but the brilliant light blinds your objecting eyes. "Who is this man," you think out loud? You stop, take a deep breath, shade your tired eyes and look with all your energy to identify the man. Still unable to do so, you strain against your fatigue and force yourself forward. "That shape, that robe, Look . . . Look . . . could it be . . . could it be the Lord," you say to yourself out loud. Then in a flash of understanding, "YES you recognize him. It is Him, how could He be here you think to yourself?" He is here in the darkness of the forest HE IS HERE! A new surge of energy reaches up from your soul and grabs your pain-racked legs. As you begin to run again toward Him He raises His hand motioning you forward. He motions his arms wide, to come to Him. As you run faster toward Him you can see that, yes it is the Lord. He raises both arms and stretches them out wide toward you . . . . He is holding our both arms wide open to welcome you. You are running as fast as you can now. Sweat is rolling down your face as you gasp for each breath of cold air. The air burns your lips as though it could tear out your throat. You duck under a low branch and trip over a root falling to your knees. You have bruised your knee and torn your pants again, but that does not matter. You get up and begin to run to our Lord again. You can see his broad loving smile now. You can see that He has begun to move toward you. Just when you think that you do not have any energy left and can not stand any longer, you fall into His arms . . . . Breathing deeply you fall gently into his strength. He folds his arms around you pulling you to him. Setting down he brings you up into his lap and pulls you close to his breast.

It's so warm there, so peaceful. You rub your face deep into His coarse robe as He grips you tightly gently rocking you. It's so good there so warm, you feel so loved, so safe and so at peace. You can hardly contain yourself as you feel His warm pulsating breath on your brow. You know now that beyond all reason and above all doubt that He truly loves you. You never want to leave Him. It is so wonderful. After a few moments of this rich goodness you feel a cold drop on your forehead. Instinctively you look up into the face of the Master. As you look up into His eyes you see great tears are running down His cheeks and striking your head. You say, "Oh Lord why do you cry?" He looks slowly into your eyes while gently rocking you and He says a with love filled half smile, "Why don't you believe I love you?"

The sounds of these words pierce your heart like a broken dagger. You raise your head from His bosom and He repeats . . . . "Why don't you believe I love you?" The words pierce your soul again. You cannot answer as your heart is clutching at your throat. You know that He is right. Ashamed, you admit to yourself that you have doubted His love many times. But you cannot say why. You cannot bare the pain of that realization. The pain wants to crush your joy and drown your peace in sorrow. You ache in the pain of that truth. You bury your face into His arms again weeping. You feel Him so close to him. He is so real and for a moment you set there weeping softly together. You know that He is real and that He does love you beyond anything that you might imagine. He wants you to have all the peace and joy of all the universe right here and right now. You feel it in your heart and wonder in your mind how such an impossible thing could be so close yet so far. So you bury your face deep into His arms, pondering his question. It's so peaceful and good there. He is so strong. You feel his warmth and all the goodness that He has to offer you there. It is good that you are there and you are at peace.

You remain there for a time consuming His love. You drink in each ray of goodness and long for the next. His presence is so real that you can taste the salt of His tears. You can feel each pounding beat of His heart as you lay your head against His chest. You can touch His warmth and know He is with you. It is good and you want it to go on forever. But He loosens His grip slightly and you cry, "No Lord, no Lord," as you push your face deeper into his bosom. He eases His grip again but you don't want Him to let go. But He gently pushes you back and says, "I love you so much. Always remember that nothing you can do can turn me away from you. I give you my solemn promise in this. I have carved your name on the palm of My hand. You are mine now I am yours." You sit there quietly as He gets up while holding you in His strong hands. Then He says, "Now sit here in the meadow and enjoy; rest among my creation and enjoy the new life I have reawakened within you," as He places you on the ground. He continues, "all that I have created on earth is here for you. Come my animals, come to me brother fawn." A small speckled fawn walks slowly out of the forest full of life and gentle. His newborn spots are so brilliant white that they seem to dance when he moves. Soon a raccoon ambles up to you and walks around your feet chattering. He curls around your arm playfully as you reach down to pet him. You bend down and scoop up a young rabbit, so soft, warm and cuddly. The fur is fuzzy and warm. As you glance over your shoulder you see the Lord at the edge of the meadow He says, "Remember me always. I am with you in all things. I have created all these things for you because I love you. I must go now, there are so many more that don't understand." And with that He's gone. He vanishes on a wisp of the wind. You remain there in the silence comforted by all of His creatures. The sun seems to have a new brilliance now as it peeks through the trees onto the meadow. Its warmth kisses you deep into your heart. It blesses your arms with warmth and goodness. Each of the animals breathes its warm breath on you filling you with their life. They by their mere existence cry out the praises of The Master's glory. You glance up as your hear the screech of a bird of pray. After a moments searching you see an eagle sailing on surly wing tips among the brilliant white clouds. With each flap of his wings he proclaims his love of life and of God. He flies up as to touch the face of God. He flies with the Master, blessing him with each beat of his wings and you know that **HE IS ALIVE!!!!!!!!!!!!!!!**

SELAH!